About the Author

Genevieve Roberts is a solo mum to her daughter Astrid. She works as a copywriter and journalist. She has written for national newspapers for fifteen years and works at a digital agency. She loves falling off surfboards and practising yoga, though at the moment she is mainly concentrating on being a mum. Genevieve currently lives in south-east London with her daughter.

GENEVIEVE ROBERTS

GOING SOLO

My choice
to become
a single mother
using a donor

piatkus

PIATKUS

First published in Great Britain in 2019 by Piatkus

1 3 5 7 9 10 8 6 4 2

A CIP catalogue record for this book
is available from the British Library.

ISBN 978-0-349-42151-3

Typeset in Bembo by M Rules
Printed and bound by CPI Group (UK) Ltd, Croydon, CR0 4YY

Papers used by Piatkus are from well-managed forests and
other responsible sources.

Piatkus
An imprint of
Little, Brown Book Group
Carmelite House
50 Victoria Embankment
London EC4Y 0DZ

An Hachette UK Company
www.hachette.co.uk

www.littlebrown.co.uk

For Astrid

Contents

Acknowledgements

Thank you to all the team at Piatkus whose work brought this book to life. Especially big thanks to Emily Arbis, whose wonderful and sensitive editing made working on my second draft a pleasure; Jo Wickham, Jillian Young and Jan Cutler.

To those behind the scenes, thank you: Harriet Walker who gave me great advice, Jen Barclay who championed the idea, Emily Dugan and Lizzy Davies, who read through initial chapters. A huge thank you to my brother Henry Roberts, who spent half his holiday giving a close read to the first draft to tell me which bits weren't working, and to my wonderful mum, who spent hours keeping Astrid entertained as I was trying to finish this book.

I want to thank the solo mum community. I'm in touch with many mothers with similar families, both by chance and through solo mum groups on social media and the Donor Conception Network, and you've all inspired me hugely.

Special thanks to all the people who've chatted to me about their experiences as solo mums, grown-ups conceived by donor sperm, and sperm donors. I've only included a fraction of the interviews because of space, but each informed this book – and my parenting of Astrid. Thanks also to the academics, doctors and fertility researchers who took the time out of their schedules to speak to me and help me understand more about fertility, and about myself.

Thank you to the wonderful colleagues who've offered me so much support along the way at the *i* paper, while I was pregnant, and at Beyond digital agency, when I returned after maternity leave. Being a solo mum would be so much harder without you.

I realised while writing this book how much it is a story of love and friendship, and I want to thank my amazing family and friends. I don't know if I'd have had the courage to try to become a solo mum without your support. So many of you have helped me hugely.

Hen, thank you for your wise advice and for never failing to make me laugh; Ma, thanks for the exceptional kindness that you show both me and Astrid; Jess, thank you for holding my hand while Astrid was delivered and for throwing her in the air when I don't dare. I know how rich I am in friends who've been a big part of my life since school and journalism college; those whom I've met at university, work, in my neighbourhood and through my brother, and how fortunate I am to have so many of you who, if ever I called in an emergency (and let there not be any on the horizon), would drop everything to be at my side. So many of you have passed on amazing clothes, toys, slings and car seats and I'm incredibly grateful. You're all so generous in sharing my happiness in everything Astrid does, and I can't thank you enough. Sarah Weaver, Chris Seymour, Ed Carpenter, Alessandra Bertini, Joe Sinclair, Petra Proitsi, thank you for making us part of your south-east London family. Lucinda Troostwyk, you appear so much throughout this book: you've supported me through a teenage miscarriage, one in my thirties and, eventually, through a pregnancy. Thank you for the friendship.

Finally, Astrid, if you read this book when you're older, I hope that each page tells of the love and joy you've added to my life. Thank you.

Prologue

Most decisions we make each day are fairly innocuous: what to eat for lunch, when to catch up with our family and friends, whether to speak up in a meeting or remain quiet. And the story of these tiny decisions becomes our lives. But sometimes we decide to do something that changes everything – one thing that means we'll never see the world, or our life, or ourselves through the same lenses ever again.

I want to recount the biggest decision I ever made and will ever make. Within six months I went from being a solo traveller on holiday in Sri Lanka to lying on a doctor's bed while a consultant inserted sperm into my vagina.

I'd always hoped to have children and had taken it utterly for granted that they would be a big part of my life. The certainty I'd felt in my teens and twenties turned to a longing in my thirties.

I was open with the people closest to me about expecting my future to involve a family – a partner and children – two things I'd never seen as separate, but rather one being a consequence of the other. But I rarely talked about the feeling of pining for this expected future. Though I'm sure most of my friends knew my hopes, I didn't acknowledge the ache I felt. Longing wasn't a feeling I was comfortable with: I had a fulfilling career; I loved going on adventures and I appreciated how lucky I was to have a carefree life. Wishing for something more felt greedy at times and futile at others.

Then people around me started having children. A ball of emotion would well up in me and I'd feel tearful, full of joy for them and feeling a complicated sense of loss myself. With close friends I'd feel a sadness that we were out of time with each other; our children would never grow up together because my children didn't exist in reality, only in my imagined future. I so desperately wanted to be a mother that I didn't want to look the subject square in the eyes because it felt overwhelming, so I tried to ignore it.

The longing for my own children didn't subside, and eventually I made a huge and wonderful decision. This is the story of how I became a solo mum, using a sperm donor. The events, feelings and smaller choices that led up to the big decision, and how it changed my life afterwards in the best possible way. It's a story of love, of friendship, of motherhood.

I've spoken to lots of people along the way: sociologists and scientists, mums and donors, children who've been conceived using donor sperm. I've learnt so much from other people's experiences – some of those stories feature within this book. I've included them when they feel most relevant, rather than strictly chronologically. And I've changed people's names if they've asked to be anonymous.

I wrote this story for anyone whose life hasn't followed the path they anticipated, as a reminder that more beauty than can be imagined may be found when life offers a surprise or a twist or a deviation from convention; when the expected gives way to make room for the most amazing things in the world to happen.

I hope this story gives hope to anyone who wants children and to anyone who finds themselves single: not to follow this path necessarily, but to remember that there are always many options.

1

Paddling Out

I wondered if I was having a midlife crisis. I was thirty-seven, single and, disconcertingly, nothing felt fulfilling in the way that it once did. I felt lacklustre and couldn't work out where the passion I felt for my job, the love for the life I'd carved out in my friendly corner of south-east London, had slipped off to.

I went away in January to escape the city lights reflecting off puddles during dark evenings, and to practise falling off surfboards in Sri Lanka. I tried to lose myself in the routine of taking a board into the tropical sea – a warm salt soup: paddling out while feeling the sun beating down on my shoulders; craning my neck to look for a wave tumbling towards the shore; then using all my arm power to propel me along the crest and attempting to get to my feet.

I'm forever a beginner surfer. I've spent so much time playing in the foamy, white water, getting ducked every time I try to take on the larger, breaking, green waves. Trying to master the skill of gliding across the swell, at the mercy of the rhythm and power of the ocean, gives a good sense of perspective. It requires concentration to have any chance of not being flung from a board, and a complete acceptance and respect that I'm not in control. And being soaked by salt water is as refreshing as it is exhausting.

I first started to spend time messing around on a surfboard when my dad was seriously ill with cancer. It stopped me worrying about him for a few seconds, as I had to focus on what was right behind me or a wave would shake me out of my thoughts and under the water. Since then, I've been drawn to waves whenever I feel emotional, and I head to the sea whenever anything significant happens in my life, whether celebrating getting together with a new boyfriend or trying to come to terms with the end of a relationship, marking the start of a new job or the end of a stale one.

Until this trip, I'd found that exploring a new country was a brilliant tonic for any twinges of discontentment in my life. It would startle me out of any rut, as I'd remember how enchanting the world is. I love meeting people whose lives aren't following the same tracks as my own, and I'd find my senses heightened by new sounds, smells and sights.

But this holiday felt different. I'm not sure whether it was despite the mix of waves and a country I'd never been to before, or because of it, but it brought into focus a lot of questions that were already on the peripheries of my mind – and that I'd remained determinedly too busy to let come out of the wings.

I was in my mid-thirties (or late thirties if you're feeling uncharitable) and was starting to consider where my life was going. At heart, perhaps I wished that I was discovering the country with someone I loved. The trip felt nothing more than a distraction from a sense of yearning. And that in itself felt frustrating: I wanted to lose myself in the sights and delights of Sri Lanka.

If I could feel unfulfilled when surrounded by lazy waves and beautiful beaches, travelling to the highlands where tea plants grew on stepped hills, then I wasn't going to be able to ignore it anywhere else. Even in paradise, things were fairly nice rather than blissful. And while fairly nice isn't a bad place to be, and life isn't always going to sparkle, I felt that something important was missing.

I'd had lots of childhood dreams: living by the sea, writing for a living and falling in love. I'd achieved my dream of becoming a writer, working for a national newspaper. I had frequent trips to the ocean in my applejack-green vintage campervan that lived on the road outside my flat, an open invitation. I knew I was incredibly fortunate. But falling in love no longer seemed so simple. And when I was growing up, I never considered that these dreams wouldn't, ultimately, involve me having children. I don't know why. The notion of having children had become an ache that was beginning to dominate my thoughts.

I'd spend huge amounts of time choosing gifts for friends' children to welcome them into the world, idly wondering what I'd choose if it were my own child. On a holiday to Mexico, I found myself buying a little white dress with people embroidered on the front because it was so beautiful. It would have fit a six-month-old. When my friend asked who it was for, I explained that it seemed that everyone I knew was having babies thick and fast, and I'd give it to the next girl to be born. Where once I'd have spent time looking round markets for clothes for myself, now I was drawn to looking at things for tiny people.

I felt that I had so much love to give, and I yearned to watch a child of my own grow and explore the world. Every time yet another friend told me that they were expecting a baby, I'd be delighted for them, but would also wonder when it would be me who would get to experience the feeling of a baby growing inside me, and then watching them grow and step towards independence. I never felt that there was a limit on the number of babies in the world or that I wanted it to be me who was pregnant instead of a friend; I just really, really wanted it to be me too. And with very close friends I would nearly say how much I'd love to be sharing this with them, going through it together. But I'd stop myself, as I understood that it could be awkward, and detract from their celebration, as they would feel the need to offer reassurance that my time would come.

I think it's a feeling that many women experience, to a greater or lesser extent.

* * *

I remember my teenage self in a high-school changing room after a game of netball, speculating with my school friends as to which of us would have children first. It wasn't a question of *if*, simply *when*. I don't think we had any awareness that having children is not always straightforward; the idea of dipping fertility would have felt so far into the future to be irrelevant. I was in serious relationships from the age of fifteen onwards, a serial monogamist, and everyone predicted I'd be the first.

Puberty hit me at thirteen during the long summer holidays, and the dose of hormones changed both the way I looked at the world and the way I looked. I had left school in July so flat-chested that I had to wear a crop top because there was nothing to put in a bra, and I returned at the beginning of September having visited Euro Disney and with breasts. I abandoned my long white socks for short black ones, and started hanging out in the bus lane before and after school, known to teenagers at the high schools in Nottingham as the designated place to develop crushes.

And those hormones helped make for some massive crushes. I didn't sleep the night after one boy held hands with me at a party; I cried in a maths lesson when my first boyfriend dumped me. Boys were a constant source of conversation during school, with days bookended by spending a few minutes chatting or kissing. I've always suspected this level of excitement over boys is something reserved for single-sex schools and it's so easy to sneer at, but it was fun to be part of. We'd plan outfits for weeks in advance of discos, where both schools got together in our assembly hall, and we would speak for weeks afterwards about who had slow-danced with whom. One girl timed the length of Bryan Adams's number-one hit '(Everything I Do) I Do It for You' because she kissed the boy she fancied for the entirety of the song, while another sparked gossip – and respect – for leading her new boyfriend behind the stage curtains for extra privacy. Any time we heard that someone fancied us, we'd almost get giddy.

Our excitement for boys remained undimmed as we first started going out to bars in town when we were fifteen and sixteen, armed with fake IDs, equalled only by the strength of our female friendships as we confided in and supported each other through our teenage years.

Whereas lots of my friends would move from boyfriend to boyfriend (two weeks felt a long time at school, and a relationship that hadn't floundered in the first month was seen as having serious potential), after a few short encounters I seemed to fall into longer-term relationships. Having a boyfriend came naturally to me: I enjoyed looking out for someone else and loved it when they were thoughtful towards me. I felt comfortable with boys, probably thanks to loving my brother's company and sharing a similar sense of humour.

I had wonderful relationships at school and at university, although at the time I had no idea how much of an effect they would have on my life decades later, or that they would help give me the confidence to make the biggest decision of my life.

I first fell in love at the beginning of my GCSE year with Richard. He had a big smile and green eyes and was two years older than me. He loved going climbing and dressed like a surfer despite never having taken a board out into waves, with Nottingham being as far away from the coast as is possible on such a small island.

He enjoyed watching adverts as much as programmes, introduced me to The Smiths, and we spoke every night on the phone. He drove to see me at weekends in a little red car at a time when being able to drive was something I admired. (When I did eventually turn seventeen I embarked on driving lessons, but found it was a skill that didn't come naturally, failing my test twice before eventually being deemed roadworthy.)

Richard had reached puberty in the 1980s, an innocent time when teenage boys who couldn't lay their hands on porn would flick through the underwear section of their mums' Freemans catalogues. And our relationship itself had an innocence that older adults patronisingly described as puppy love.

On Richard's last day of school before sitting his A levels, he and his friends dressed as Reservoir Dogs, walking through the school without a hint of menace between them. When our A levels and GCSEs were over, we spent the post-exam summer together lying in gardens, relaxing after all the studying, celebrating results – both believing, as so many other teenagers are convinced each year, that the distance between us when he went to university wouldn't matter. Despite our best efforts, it did. It was my first experience that love doesn't always last forever, and how easy it is to get caught up in new experiences. I suspect it added to my insecurities, and made me want to grasp tighter to love when it came along.

Then, in my first year at Leeds University, I fell deeply in love with Ross, a teenager from Cardiff who gradually became friends with me and used to come and visit me and the four girls I lived with. He asked me to cut his long hair, but I didn't know he had a crush on me – until one night, when he kissed me. Every evening afterwards, for months, he'd turn up at the flat, and stay over in my single bed. We'd spend long nights out drinking with our friends, or chatting to my flatmates, and long mornings in bed. We never made a plan to see each other – I didn't have a mobile. Then one night he didn't come and see me. I realised I had kept listening out for his arrival and – when it didn't come – just how much I missed him. When I saw him again the next day, I realised that I was falling in love.

We'd go on trips to the Yorkshire Moors to walk in the countryside and to Bradford to eat curries with the biggest naan bread I've ever seen. We stayed together all the way through university, through huge fights where I'd call and call afterwards until he'd eventually pick up the phone, through the insecurity of one of his friends frequently trying to kiss him, through our final exams.

After university, we both stayed at my mum's for a few months while we saved money to go travelling: we worked in a call centre during the day, booking lecturers to cover courses, and served guests at a tapas restaurant at night.

By November, we'd earned enough money to spend six months exploring India. I'd never been outside Europe before. We flew into Calcutta, and the assault on my senses was so overwhelming that after a day exploring the flower market I fell soundly asleep. I awoke to the smell of smoke. 'Fire! Fire!' I screamed, as I ripped our mosquito net apart. Ross jumped out of bed and realised almost immediately that it was a family cooking their breakfast on the street outside.

I loved the sensory bombardment of India and we were both enchanted by the country.

In the past I'd always felt a little in Ross's shadow. He had so much energy that he cartwheeled round supermarkets, DJ'd at clubs where sweat ran off the walls and was so sociable he seemed to know hundreds of people at university. But while travelling I started to feel more self-assured – more me, not just Ross's girlfriend. Being with him felt like home, and that sense of safety helped my confidence to grow.

Backpacking on a budget is essentially an extended holiday with more stomach bugs, with acres of amazing time to write and explore – and even to sand and polish pieces of coconuts to make hair clips. There's enough time to fall out too. After forty-eight hours on a train travelling from Bangalore in the south of India to Allahabad in the far north, we were stinking and overtired, and had a huge row. We went out to find some food and stormed around the town in furious moods, but then we stumbled across a wedding party dancing on the street. We were dragged in to join the dancing, and I was pulled up on top of an elephant leading a procession. 'This is why I love you,' shouted Ross. It was a good way to end an argument.

We caught the tail end of the Kumbh Mela in Allahabad, the biggest religious festival in the world, where millions of Indians gather to wash away a lifetime of sins in an increasingly filthy confluence of the Ganges. We went to see the Dalai Lama in McLeod Ganj, visited the hill station of Darjeeling where tea is grown, and Rishikesh, the yoga capital of the world, and we spent time on Goan beaches where cows wander between the palm trees along the sand.

After India, we carried on travelling through south-east Asia and stopped in a town called Beihai in southern China where we had jobs teaching English. We learnt to make dumplings, tried (and in my case failed) to master the language and played pool with new friends.

When our travels ended we moved to a flat in White-chapel in east London with a ladder up to the rooftop, where we spent long spring evenings looking out on to the street below, in air scented with the amazing spices from the Punjabi restaurant Tayyabs opposite. Its walls were adorned with famous people who'd eaten there; its kebabs and bring-your-own policy made it our favourite place to eat in London. But while we loved our corner of east London, day-to-day life started to weigh heavily on our relationship.

I'd sent off dozens of letters to get work experience at newspapers, and work took the place that exploring had held for the previous couple of years. After weeks of work experience in newsrooms, I was finally offered an official role. I wanted to be successful so much that I found starting my first proper job stressful. I loved my days; I enjoyed learning about the newspaper industry and found my colleagues listened to my ideas and encouraged me to write. But after work, I'd find it easy to worry whether I was doing okay, whether I'd missed an important email, or whether there were errors in what I'd written.

Our arguments became mundane, about cleaning the bathroom or washing up. I'd look around hopefully for a wedding procession led by an elephant to help distract us. My head was whirring. I was naive and didn't realise that love – the kind that I'd experienced twice, where you find a best friend – is rare and not something to take for granted. And I ended it.

I married my next boyfriend, despite having doubts, in my late twenties. We got together when I was feeling lonely. I missed Ross hugely. I found Tim challenging, his opinions almost always contradicted my own. He represented the transition from carefree youth to adulthood for me: whereas Ross would happily talk about musical beats per minute (which I knew nothing about), Tim was more comfortable talking about the world (which I also knew nothing about, but I was learning and felt I could share my views). He was an established journalist, embedded in a world I'd just come into, with tales to share about an industry I'd fallen in love with.

I wanted to soften him with love.

We worked different hours and I always felt very insecure about our relationship, though I'm not really sure why. He had opinions on everything, from wine and cheese to the latest developments in Iraq. He was so self-assured that sometimes I felt that he was from a completely different generation from me; there was still so much I couldn't be certain about. In reality, it was just four years separating us.

He cooked me dinner when he wasn't working and would send me text messages with simply a kiss when I was out with my friends.

Everything moved so rapidly, and within months we were living together, and a year later had bought a place together. Even so, I hadn't thought of our future in a forever type of way. Not that I thought that we wouldn't grow old together, just that I was in my mid-twenties and it took all my efforts to keep up with the present, let alone throwing the future into the mix. I didn't think about growing old, full stop.

His marriage proposal left me slack-jawed for days. We

were at a Beautiful and the Damned party. I'd dressed as a 1920s' flapper girl; he was dressed as a devil, covered in red face paint. There was no down-on-one-knee, more an, 'I've been trying to ask this for ages' in a corner.

'Yes, but please ask me again in the morning,' I said. 'Please don't tell anyone now.'

A friend came over and he turned to her and said: 'You can be the first to know.' We'd both been drinking and he probably didn't process what I was saying. Even after several glasses of rum, I thought the sobriety of morning would be a good measure of whether we were both serious about this. But somehow once it became public, it felt harder to reconsider.

We were very different souls, and as we got to know each other that became clearer. I had spent roughly one month from the age of fifteen to twenty-five single. I met him when he was comfortable as a single man, and I think he understandably felt that being in a couple inevitably involved a level of compromise, a sacrifice of freedom.

I loved sharing my life and slotting into other people's. Because I was so used to it, I didn't really understand how much people value their independence, nor that it's perfectly natural to miss big swathes of time where you do exactly as you please. I enjoyed it when Ross came with me to visit my family, and I loved his family and looked forward to trips to his home town. I expected that I'd experience that again with Tim, but like so many people, my new fiancé (the word feels as awkward to me now as it did then) didn't seem to share the same excitement over visiting his in-laws. He begrudged time away from friends in London.

On one occasion, I was coming home from work after midnight from a late shift, and I passed by Camden in north London where he'd been out with friends, and had said he was about to head home. 'I'm in a cab, I'll come by and we can travel home together,' I told him, thinking I was doing something thoughtful. Instead, he seemed frustrated and resentful that I didn't leave him to get to our home about half an hour away under his own steam. I spent days stewing over why he wasn't happy for comfort and to save the need for public transport. It was only years later, when I'd grown used to being single, that I could even start to see that perhaps he felt that I was taking his independence rather than looking out for him.

In the weeks before our wedding I asked to postpone it, but he said no. On the morning of the ceremony my mouth was so dry that I couldn't eat. People were drinking champagne but I couldn't swallow properly. Tim later told me that my smile looked fake as I walked towards him in the register office. At the reception, one of his friends told me how wonderful marriage is, how it feels so secure and settled. I thought to myself: *But I don't feel either secure or settled.* Perhaps I just didn't know him well enough, or perhaps I felt scared because I'd been ignoring concerns for far too long.

My doubts continued through our one year of marriage. We fought so much that my neighbours got in touch to check everything was okay. I felt I'd made a terrible mistake to get married without feeling certain. The friendship I'd completely taken for granted in previous relationships wasn't there: we'd try to communicate and end up arguing; we seemed unable to be supportive of one another. Perhaps we were just too different, and the initial burst of opposites attracting had turned to friction and frustration. Before I turned thirty, I told him I wanted a divorce.

This was not a life error I'd ever expected to make. Worse than losing trust in other people, I stopped trusting my own judgement. My parents had divorced when I was fourteen, and I was determined that when I got married it would be for life. I regretted that I'd made too many serious relationship decisions at breakneck speed and had ended up hurting other people and myself.

After that, I became exceptionally cautious about relationships. I went to Paris for a year. I'd made some terrible mistakes in London. I told my friends I wanted to fall in love with a place rather than a person.

Before I left for Paris, I started seeing a man from Sheffield who was friends with a couple of my friends when they were growing up. It was so soon after my marriage had ended that I hadn't considered future relationships, serious or not – and this could easily have been a brief but enjoyable distraction.

Seth would have been in the year above me at school, a status that would have felt so important when we were half our current age. We wandered through Margate, where he now lived, watched paragliders on the South Downs, and walked around Westminster, stopping in pubs. He filled an iPod with music for me to take across the Channel, the modern version of a mix tape. We texted almost constantly for the first month I was away, but after one visit he told me he didn't want a long-distance relationship. I played a tune that reminded me of him hundreds of times over the next weeks and sobbed as if I were a heartbroken teenager, but he didn't get back in touch. It had the hallmarks of a fling consigned to history, one that I'd possibly remember once in a while and wonder idly what had happened to that man with the romantic gestures who filled the gap between my married and single life. I couldn't have imagined, when I was living around the corner from the Beaubourg in Paris, what an important but unlikely part in my life he'd come to play.

After Seth, boyfriends became fewer and further

between – I wanted to make sure that I didn't make any more errors. My housemate suggested that I get a sleeping dictionary – a French boyfriend – so that I could improve my language. But aside from a couple of French kisses, I was content trying to speak to everyone in a city that I could walk the length of, where I'd spend mornings in coffee shops, working at my computer, and evenings drinking kir with friends.

A year later, I returned to the UK still feeling slightly bruised, but wanting to root myself in a country surrounded by people I love. I was coming back increasingly frequently as so many of my friends were getting married, and I didn't want to miss out on such important life events.

I received an email from my sister-in-law, Jess, suggesting that now was the right time for me to move back, and that I should move to south London. It sounded like a good idea. I didn't know that she was pregnant.

I felt hugely emotional when my sister-in-law told me that she and my brother were expecting a baby. I was delighted that I was soon to become an auntie, but, as the slightly older sister, I was used to experiencing rites of passage just before my brother: university, jobs, marriage. But not this. I told myself that I was pleased the attention wasn't channelled towards me – my family were so excited that I thought it might feel overwhelming – but there was a little bit of me that felt a pang that I wasn't the one experiencing pregnancy. It was a complicated melancholy, because I was so very happy for them. I wanted desperately to have the chance to have a baby, but I could afford to be patient.

Eight weeks after returning, my dad was diagnosed with cancer. My brother and I would coordinate our visits with my aunt, Bron, to time with chemotherapy and radiotherapy sessions so that he never had to go to hospital alone. All my caring, maternal instincts were activated by my dad getting sick. I wanted more than anything to help him get better. When people asked how I was, I'd tell them how my dad was doing.

And then my nephew William was born: I was overwhelmed by a magical love. I spent so much time with him, visiting, playing, cuddling. Often when I was with him I felt the ache of longing to become a parent myself, but these feelings were dwarfed by the adoration I felt for him; the pride in watching him grow and start to explore the world. I'd often have tears in my eyes as I felt almost overwhelmed by love, grief that my dad was dying, and a realisation that I could no longer take it for granted that I'd have children of my own. And if I looked at all glum, he'd show me so much affection that I'd be pulled back to the joy of the present, where I got to play with this amazing boy.

The next year was tough, supporting my dad through an aggressive operation that almost eradicated the uninvited cells. He woke up from the surgery, distressed, in pain and asked how he looked. There was no mirror to show him, so I offered to take a photo. At that moment, a cheerful nurse came past and insisted on putting her arm around my dad for the photo. It was one of the most awkward pictures I've taken. And her celebratory demeanour later seemed misplaced: although the doctors had hoped that they had removed all the sinister cells they found traces of the cancer still present. I'll always feel grateful that we had time to play hundreds of games of chess together (I always lost, even when he was very ill indeed). My brother Henry, my aunt and I got to spend lots of time with my dad, whose obsession and delight with food grew as eating became increasingly painful. We laughed at his requests for ice-cream combinations that might be for sale in the best gelaterias in Italy but aren't readily available in Nottingham; his rhapsodies over toffee pavlova and his theory that McDonald's had very deliberately set out to corner the market of people who want to eat but have lost their teeth. I went on a nostalgic trip with him to the country fair at Abergavenny, his childhood home in Wales, where there was still an annual garden-on-a-plate competition. And, at a time when the doctors would have expected him to be bed-bound, he travelled to London and I witnessed his pride and delight at meeting my nephew, who shared his name, William.

As autumn arrived, my dad became weaker, faded and died.

My brother Henry and I arranged the funeral, shocked and numbed by this expected departure. We collected some of the poems my dad had written so that if people took away the order of service they'd also take something dear to him. In between his favourite music, the tunes he'd play on the piano when we were children, I went up to the front to speak about my dad's character and what he meant to me. There was a moment when my voice cracked and I didn't know whether I was about to sob my heart out, but somehow, it passed and I was able to talk about the games he played when we were young children, letting us climb up his legs so that we could practise somersaults, and balance across his feet so that we could be flying angels. I talked about how he had explained the world to us in his serious voice; his obsessions, from bamboo to his childhood home in Wales; his impatience with those slower than him.

My dad loved horse racing and we held his wake at Nottingham Racecourse. Family friends came along to show their support. There was food and drinks, but the only thing I can remember were sticky, cloyingly sweet honey-glazed cocktail sausages. Henry and I laid flowers at the winning post in honour of our dad.

I felt lost in life and lost in relationships. I was grieving throughout my dad's illness, and grieving after he died.

Jess was soon pregnant again, and I found it more straightforward the second time, perhaps because this was completely expected. It hadn't crossed my mind that my brother and she wouldn't have a second child. When Dylan arrived, my heart expanded again. I didn't think it was possible to love anyone more than these two boys: I'd visit and babysit and play. It's an incredibly special role to get to be an auntie, a privilege to always indulge and entertain. No amount of confusion over my own life showing no sign of following the path I hoped for would stop me from spending time with my nephews.

*   *   *

Soon after I returned from Paris, I thought Ross and I were getting back together. We went together to a screening of a film that a friend had made, a comedy about a group of tourists on a bus trip round India, and as we kissed, so briefly, as we were saying goodbye, I felt that this was our second chance. But the next time I heard from him he'd met someone else. At first, I felt disbelief: hadn't he realised that now was our time? And then I felt a growing sense of loss. A few months later, I spent a long-haul flight on an almost empty plane lying across three seats, crying as I realised that our moment had passed, feeling that I'd messed up. Our orbits were never to overlap again.

My formative relationships had been with people who were initially friends, and I found the same happening again. Perhaps it felt safer to date someone whom I already felt was supportive of me and I of them, though I learnt that being friends with someone before getting into a relationship with them is no insurance against getting hurt. But I suspect that there was a part of me that felt that a relationship was likely to move faster if I already knew the person.

There's a very subtle shift in relationships between teens and twenties, compared with thirties. No one warned me about it, and it was as unexpected as it is logical. Simply, the older people get, the more likely they are to run into commitment-phobes when dating. In our teens and twenties, those who are comfortable in serious relationships gradually meet someone who they want to travel through life with. It tends to be those who are commitment-shy, or who prefer being single, who are still enjoying dating in their thirties. A friend said he noticed this starkly in his life; it was at the age of twenty-nine he suddenly found all his mates were in partnerships. Which means navigating dating in your thirties – certainly in a city like London where lots of people do enjoy being single and are overwhelmed by choice – is trickier.

There are obvious exceptions to this because not all relationships last. But many a serial monogamist will go straight into their next relationship with barely time to catch breath and look around. And until I'd shaken myself so very badly by getting married and divorced in quick succession, my relationship pattern was similar; I simply preferred having a partner.

Some of my friends used to delight in collecting funny dating stories and would dine out on tales of disastrous evenings. I was the opposite. I'd happily swap tales of meeting new men for trusting someone and being in a secure relationship with them. Which is fitting, because the first time I spent any length of time single, in my early thirties, I learnt that I was catastrophically bad at dating. Grief for my dad made the world seem a dimmer place, anyway, but it wasn't that. It was more that there was an insouciance among daters in London that I hadn't acquired over the years.

I showed myself up as an amateur very quickly. My naivety was clear when I kissed a friend one night at a wedding in

Wales. We knew each other; we fancied each other. I presumed that would mean we'd go straight into a relationship. At breakfast the next morning, I put his lack of affection down to our hangovers. I simply didn't understand that a kiss wasn't something that could be read into. We drove back from north Wales to London together. I felt that if we could last a long journey like that and still have things to chat about, we were well on our way to becoming boyfriend and girlfriend. A relationship probably hadn't crossed his mind.

I sent texts suggesting we meet up, and would check my phone for a response. Often I'd hear nothing for twenty-four hours. We went to the cinema a few times and kissed again, before I realised that he simply wasn't that interested in having a relationship with me.

For the next few years I continued dating friends, and if I met someone I fancied I'd try to become friends with them first, all, I suspect, in the misguided hope that it offered a shield against hurt.

It all felt so much trickier than when I was a teenager: the boys I met then had to be prepared to navigate phoning my home and making small talk with my mum to get to speak to me in the evening. The effort was so much greater than with men who would now rely on text messages, and consequently there were fewer misunderstandings.

Perhaps it's not surprising that when I took a step away from my London life, went on holiday far away and looked at it from a distance, I started asking myself where my life was going. I was rich in friendships and family, whom I treasure, and I didn't have any concerns about my career. I knew I had so much to feel grateful for, but finding a lasting relationship felt as elusive as it did important to me. I hadn't got further than false starts, and it felt as if the more I wanted to find a partner, the more likely love was to elude me. Not only did I want to experience the feeling of being in love again, of sharing my life with someone, I also wanted to try to have children. I felt a million miles away from the life I wanted to be leading, and didn't know how to take the first step towards the family I so wished for.

2

Taking Measure

I spent my fortnight in Sri Lanka reflecting on my life, and, over the course of the holiday, I decided that it was time to take action. I'd always assumed that I would be in a loving relationship before having a family. But it felt time to consider these two hugely important future wishes separately. I'd come away to play around on surfboards, so it surprised me that by the end of my holiday I was ready to explore the idea of starting a family, regardless of not being in love.

On the last day of my holiday I messaged a single friend, Tristan, who had recently adopted a daughter. I wanted to find out more about his journey to becoming a father; perhaps I should be following in his footsteps and putting my name down on the adoption register.

On my return to the UK, we spoke about his decisions. We spoke one evening, after his daughter was in bed. He was honest about how tough it is to adopt in the UK,

despite measures being put in place to help make the process smoother.

'I was one of the lucky ones,' he said of his two-year wait.
He was looking to adopt a child, rather than a baby, where
the competition is even tougher. He told me how difficult
it is even when you reach the top of the adoption list. In his
case several prospective parents had been interviewed before
a decision was made as to which would gain a daughter.

It sounded so brutal. Although no one working in the
adoption services has ever intended it to be so, I felt he was
describing the most ruthless competition, with a child as
the prize.

The other people hoping to adopt a child were all couples.
As a brilliant primary school teacher, I wasn't surprised that
he'd been successful.

When I told him I was considering also trying to become
a single parent, he asked my age, and urged me to get
on with it.

'If I were a woman, I'd have tried to make one myself.
Don't leave it too late,' he told me.

He was adamant that adoption is a very hard way around,
and only made sense to him because he can't carry a baby,
and was more interested in adopting a child anyway.

Despite his wish to be a father – he'd put his relationships
on hold for the previous two years so that he could concentrate on getting through the hoops of adoption – he warned
me that being a parent alone wasn't easy. 'If you're on your
own, however much support you've got from family and
friends, there will be things that you're really excited about
that other people just aren't as interested in,' he told me. 'The
little details; new words. You're cheering your child along,
but there's no one there to cheer with you.'

He said he'd never wished more that he had a partner who

he could share his daughter's little wins with. Despite this, he adored being a dad, loved watching his daughter gain in confidence as she grew and was convinced he'd made the right decision: he had no regrets about becoming a parent.

Tristan's evident happiness made me feel hopeful. Despite his reminder that time was of the essence (he might even have used the dreaded description 'biological clock'), I still had my high-school changing-room confidence that fertility was nothing for me to be concerned about. But I wanted to know for sure, so I did what an increasing number of people do in my position and went to have my fertility tested.

A swift search of fertility clinics in London brought up a selection of private clinics, all happy to scan a woman's ovaries for a fee. I picked one with a name that I liked and went to see a gynaecologist.

I'd been pregnant before, almost two years earlier, and as it was unintentional, I believed it suggested that I was unusually fertile. My real worry was whether or not I could carry a child: I had learnt the hard way that having a baby isn't always as simple as meeting him or her nine months after you become pregnant.

My first miscarriage was as a teenager. Richard and I were in love, we were young and desperately naive. It was when he was at university and I was still at school – and we were attempting a long-distance relationship where he called at 6.00pm each night to catch up – that I'd found out I was pregnant. (I'd have just finished watching *Neighbours* after a day studying for A levels; he was living in halls and enjoying not studying.)

I did a pregnancy test that was negative, but my period was late, so while in town one Saturday with friends, I went to the health centre. They confirmed what I'd suspected.

I felt shame and sadness, but overall it seemed very surreal.

I don't think I considered having the baby properly; it seemed impossible for me to have a child then. I felt I'd have crushed my family's dreams – I was on tight train tracks that were leading to the door of a university, and I didn't question or try to stop the ride.

I told my then-boyfriend, and he said that a part of him was proud. I don't think he really considered that I was going to have the baby either.

I remember thinking my belly had become bigger (although that could easily have been in my mind), and, as the pregnancy hormones began to play their part, I started having fleeting thoughts about what would happen if I did have the baby. Was there a possible way?

Then, I started spotting, out in town on a Saturday evening. The following night I had bad period cramps all night. On Monday morning, on my way to school, I haemorrhaged, and I had blood staining my black stretch jeans. My friend Lucinda had recently passed her driving test and took me back home. I sat on a ripped-up cardboard box in her car so that I didn't stain the seats of her Renault Clio.

When I look back on it now, I remember how overwhelming it felt for me, but I'm sure it was for her too, however grown up we felt at sixteen. This wasn't the same kind of fear as going into a test we'd forgotten to revise enough for. On an average school day, our main preoccupations (aside from studying) were finding good seats in the common room and spending the dinner money our parents gave us each day on lemonade and chips for lunch in the pub by our school because the barman was good-looking. But Lucinda was kind and thoughtful (which she always is) and stayed with me and checked I was okay.

Miscarriage wasn't something I understood, or knew

how to cope with. And for all her kindness and support, I suspect it may be one of Lucinda's darker memories too. I remember we called the women's health clinic in the afternoon to say there was still blood; they had to explain that it was to be expected, miscarriages last longer than a morning, and that I was fine unless there was another haemorrhage.

I was due to take part in the final of a public-speaking competition in Edinburgh a couple of days later. Schools put forward teams of three people who compete against each other. I'd written and practised my speech, and our team had got through several rounds to make it to the final. I didn't feel that I could go. I was still bleeding, so, in tears, I told my mum. She was very shocked and upset that I hadn't told her I was pregnant so that she could have offered me support. Even though I was no longer pregnant, I suspect that nightmare images of me as a teen mum might have flashed before her eyes. She was sympathetic but firm: I had to go to Edinburgh. At the time, her approach to any crisis or heartache was to throw herself into work. And she suggested that I did the same. I know that she felt that distraction was the kindest way to deal with trauma. It didn't stop it being a miserable trip, and I found I couldn't lose myself in public speaking or studying or anything. I wanted to be hugging my boyfriend Richard, or at home curled up in bed. Most of all, I didn't want to pretend everything was okay. It was a relief to get home a couple of days later.

A week later, I had a hospital appointment to check that there was no tissue still inside me. I'd had a complete miscarriage, meaning that there was nothing remaining of the baby that could have been. Physically, the experience was over. Emotionally, I was a mess for the rest of sixth form. I worked hard enough to get good grades, but I couldn't just bury the trauma, and it wasn't until I went to university that I came to terms with what had happened and was able to move on.

But compared with my next miscarriage, the first left no scars. I was thirty-five the second time I miscarried, and it came at the end of the most unpredictable summer. I remember it as if it were now.

* * *

It's been five years since I first went out with Seth, and we're dating again. We get together once more in the autumn, but by Christmas he has withdrawn. He gets back in touch in spring, and we've been out for meals, drinks.

I buy a pregnancy test, just to reassure myself. Shock, disbelief jolts through me – I don't understand how I can be pregnant. The timing makes no sense. Does he have some kind of super-strength sperm? We aren't in a stable relationship and I spend a day trying to process the news, crying to myself, working out what I want, or rather what I don't want – an abortion – before talking to him.

He says he doesn't want to end this pregnancy either, and we decide that we'll give things a go. I suggest that a strong friendship is a good way to give a child security and stability, and that there is no pressure on us to be a couple. I write it to him in an email. I keep thinking that I don't want him to be with me only because of a baby: he'd be doing both me and the baby a disservice.

Seth starts to stay over frequently; he is thoughtful and charming and funny. There's something very youthful about him, although it might partly be that I remember him as a pal of my friends when we were teenagers.

We go out for dinners and I watch him playing tennis. I lie in bed at night and think his face, framed by almost-black hair, has a beauty to it. I feel swollen with pregnancy, hormonal and exhausted. We take my campervan over to le Touquet in north France with a group of friends, but I mainly feel nauseous. A friend tells me that she can tell I'm pregnant because Seth is so attentive.

We send each other hundreds of emails; a constant conversation where we're sharing our interests at that time (me: Peter Cook; him: invites to lectures on Thomas Cromwell). I'm enchanted.

He invites me on his family holiday to Portugal. One night, as we wander through the village with a fireworks display in the background, I feel as if I'm in a fairy tale. At other times, I feel insecure: we've gone from dating to serious relationship almost overnight. But we've been in each other's lives, however distantly, for such a long time that I try to relax. He's not a complete stranger. I find pregnancy hormones make me emotional and I'll usually cry, for very little reason, for about ten minutes a day and then I'll be completely fine. Seth seems to find this frustrating, so I Google 'pregnancy-crying' and show him the scores of articles that come up.

I return home a few days ahead of him, and when he flies back he comes straight to my flat, with gifts of a tiny music box and a metal heart-shaped container with a stone dipped in lavender essential oil. He tells me that he's fallen in love with me. I tell him I love him.

We have sex and I notice a little bit of blood on my sheets; I'm spotting. It's not dramatic. He asks to move in and live with me. A part of me feels a bit more secure about our relationship. I might be losing a baby and he now wants to live with me, so he must care about me even if we lose our child. We both have a sleepless night. We'd been planning a long lie-in on the Sunday before heading to Margate. By seven in the morning, we're both restless and decide to check what's going on.

Accident and Emergency departments are funny places
early on a Sunday morning. It's too early in the day for
anyone but insomniacs to have injured themselves from
over-enthusiastic DIY. The waiting room is almost empty,
and there appear to be few doctors around too. But I am
seen by a reassuring medic who takes a blood test and sends
me for a scan.

There is a heartbeat. The baby is six weeks in size. I feel a
little confused, as I'm eight weeks pregnant, but the doctor
seems relaxed and asks us to come back in a fortnight.

For those two weeks there's a gulf between my uncon-
scious and conscious mind. I know something isn't right. But
I so desperately want everything to be okay that listening to
reassurances is helpful. Seth is incredibly thoughtful and listens patiently to all my concerns. He even sends me Robert
Burns's poem 'Oh Wert Thou in the Cauld Blast' and tells
me it makes him think of me. (I've never had a boyfriend
who would send me poems before; I didn't know that sort
of thing really happened.)

He moves bags of his stuff into my flat, and I clear out half
my wardrobe for him.

Everything is going to be cool – I am just worrying.

We go to a friend's wedding; he's pissed off that I want
him to come. I feel vulnerable and start worrying that I'm
being needy and annoying.

Two weeks later, and we return to the hospital. The worst
scan – no heartbeat. A missed miscarriage. Seth hugs me.
'I love you, I love you, I love you, I love you, I love you,'
repeating it as if he could undo the sadness with affection.

The next hours and days are a blur.

His tears; sitting on Telegraph Hill.

The incredible pain of miscarrying. Tablets are placed
inside my vagina to force the baby out of me. Within hours,

I start feeling the waves of pain. It gets so bad that I stagger from my lounge to lie down, curled up, on my bed. Just at the point where it feels unbearable, when I apparently turn completely pale, it subsides.

Seth brushes my hair afterwards.

The days following are tough. I feel lost, pregnancy hormones still swirling through my body. I lean on him very hard. We book a holiday to the west coast of France for three weeks later, so that we can relax after too much intensity. I cancel work for a couple of weeks; getting through each day is as much as I can manage, and I don't even know if I'm doing that okay. I tell Seth I want to be pregnant again; he starts to disagree. We don't have a proper conversation about it; perhaps we're both too raw to speak properly.

After a few days, Seth returns to his research work as a biologist. On his first day, he says he watches a train pass by on the platform and forgets to board it. I wonder if he's relieved to leave the oppressiveness of the flat: the lounge where I'd started miscarrying; the bed where I lay in pain as contractions wracked my body.

We take the campervan to the Sussex countryside at the weekend and walk around a sculpture park. I start feeling calmer, I stop reliving the contractions – it's good to be surrounded by green.

I have a hospital appointment to check whether I've miscarried completely. I have and don't need an operation. I go to the cinema with my nephews. Just as we're leaving, Seth calls me.

'I'll call you back when you're not with your nephews,' he says.

I get home, and he calls me to say he doesn't want to be a parent with me.

'That's okay,' I say.

'No, it isn't okay,' he tells me angrily.

'I don't understand: are you telling me you don't want to be a parent, or you don't want to be with me?'

'Aren't they the same thing?'

'No,' I tell him. 'We need to meet up.'

'Not now,' he says.

And that's it. He doesn't come back to mine. I feel the plug being pulled out of my world, my life swirling out of my belly button. I'm like an animal, pacing round and round my flat with compounded grief.

He's grieving too. It must be overwhelming for him. Perhaps he feels he's had some kind of breakdown.

Wrapped up in loss, post-pregnancy hormones swilling, it takes all my effort to keep myself together through each day. I see him once more, when he comes to pick up all his boxes of belongings that he'd moved to my flat with enthusiasm so recently.

'There's so much,' he says, sounding surprised.

Those hormones take weeks to subside, and I am caught in limbo, regretting things I hadn't done and said and asked. Just surviving. Wishing his feelings for me hadn't changed. Perhaps he'd fallen in love with the package – me plus future child – rather than me for who I am. And when I'm not thinking about Seth, I'm thinking about our baby. What might have been. It's like living in a shadow state, halfway between being a mother and not a mother, never having got to meet my child. Even at ten weeks, I'd grown to love this tiny blob that we called Avocado. It crosses my mind that if I'd never told Seth that I was pregnant, I'd be in a stronger place. But that would have been dishonest, so I can't regret that.

A good friend whom I've known since school has given birth to her daughter just days before I miscarried, and my brother buys gifts for me to send. There's no way I can go into a baby shop; the pain is too raw. I'm enveloped in a grief for what I've lost, but also for a future that has vanished.

My friend Sarah, who is off on maternity leave while I am at my lowest, brings her new son along to meet me and pretty much ignores him while listening to my desperation. I've grown used to interrupted conversations with friends when there are children around, but somehow she is determined not to let this happen: if she even acknowledges her son it is with an eye roll or a suggestion that he's slightly annoying. It must have taken monumental strength from her to defy every instinct and decide that in that moment my needs are greater than those of her tiny, new son. It's a huge act of friendship.

As time goes on, the raw panic subsides and I get used to a constant background whirr of loss. I could watch films on top of it, have conversations with friends. I must have appeared always slightly distracted.

Soon, I hear that Seth has met a new girlfriend. I wonder whether he ever thinks of what could have been.

'I lost myself,' I tell my friend Lucinda weeks later, when I feel thoroughly miserable and, in the gloom of loss, responsible for Seth leaving. It's the second miscarriage that she's supported me through. I'd turned to her, my brother and sister-in-law in panic on the night that Seth had left.

'But you need someone who will help you find yourself when you lose your way, not who leaves you lost,' she says.

Transporting the shell of my body around, I feel stifled on the Tube, and can feel my windpipe compressed in the crowds. I'm not tired of London, but I feel assaulted by it and I avoid the centre of the city. Millions of people dressed in dark jackets feel aggressive, impersonal, exhausting. I crave horizons. Green. Calm. The corduroy stripes of the sea. My friend Emily suggests we take my van on a trip to north

Devon. It feels good to get my wetsuit on, to mess around in the water and to be knocked by tiny waves. That evening, we cook bananas and chocolate wrapped in foil over a fire pit while our towels dry on the side of the campervan, over-looking Putsborough beach. It's the first night since losing my baby that I sleep.

*   *   *

I tell all my close friends about my second miscarriage. I hadn't mentioned that I was pregnant, and catching people up suddenly on a surprise pregnancy that lasted ten weeks but had left me broken felt harder than inviting them along on the journey in the first place. They carried me with their support. The taboo surrounding the first months of any pregnancy, and all-too-frequent miscarriages, felt so misplaced in my situation when I didn't, any longer, have a partner to talk to about it. Perhaps one day, for those who wish for it, private grief will be replaced by openness, love and support.

Eventually, I come to terms with the sadness, and slowly, so gradually, I regain my trust in the world. I've always treasured friendships, but I am more aware than ever that love and support makes the world go round.

Now, at the fertility clinic one and a half years later, I hope that I'll be given results that mean I can happily put my dreams of children to the back of my mind until I am in a serious relationship, knowing that my biology has written them into my future.

I feel nervous having my ovaries scanned. I watch the obstetrician cover the wand in gel before inserting it into my vagina, and then giving me an ultrasound very similar to one that many women experience in the first weeks of pregnancy. It's not painful, although intrusive. I can see my ovaries appearing on her screen. She tells me that there are a small number of follicles that are producing eggs, which suggests that I am not infertile.

I have a blood test taken and wait a fortnight for the results that will put my mind at ease. The blood test is to check my anti-müllerian hormone levels, a hormone that starts high and drops throughout a woman's adult life, ending in zero during the menopause.

My levels are emailed to me one Friday afternoon after a brief phone call. They don't suggest low fertility – they have come in *below* that. The consultant might have seen follicles on my ovaries, but it sounds as if these were some of my last, like the late-stayers at a party which I hadn't realised was coming to an end, already a bit worse for wear.

I cry, but I only half-believe it. Perhaps it's the pink signature from the obstetrician that makes the results feel amateur, or my journalist's suspicion that this is a money-making business – especially as the obstetrician has urged me to try IVF swiftly. Or perhaps it is simply shock at a complete contradiction of my world view.

The weekend after receiving the results the news starts to sink in. I feel shattered, and am at a good friend's hen do. Her best women has hired a house in the countryside outside Bristol, but I bow out early, leaving because I don't want to get drunk and find that I am sobbing my heart out. I explain to the organisers why I am leaving, and they are incredibly sympathetic and helpful. I feel such a sense of relief: if anything like this had happened in my twenties I'd have given some excuse, feigned a headache, to leave. But with age I have the confidence to be more open, and in return I see more people open up to me.

I learn from one of the organisers about her recent

experience of having her eggs frozen – something she found intrusive and unpleasant, she said – and she talks to me about different fertility clinics around London.

I take her advice on clinics and decide to take control.

I've never really understood that fertility is inclined to sneak away unexpectedly. After splitting up with someone at thirty it didn't cross my mind to start dating swiftly because of fertility: none of my friends had children, so perhaps that made it feel distant. It was something I knew I wanted, but there didn't seem to be any rush.

Within a couple of years, I was surrounded by friends with their babies, and I started noticing headlines about threats to sperm, from laptops, hormones in rivers, even cycling, and fertility 'dropping off a cliff after the age of thirty-five'. Cruel timing: I was ready to have children, I had been for years, but I was no closer to being in love.

It's almost as if I learnt too late, but perhaps I'm one of a generation who have understood the limits of our fertility belatedly: a generation of women who have felt free to pursue careers and passions; a generation that has made the most of friendships and travelling, and explored what is important to them as well as discovering the world around them. A generation that has suffered as they learnt that people can have it all, but not necessarily at the same time – and that the order counts too. I've never once heard a woman without children talk about any limits to their career (which is not to say that there's gender equality yet, but more that women are free to follow their ambitions), but it's a frequent conversation among those with children. I'm one of many people who wasn't truly aware of deadlines (or at least those outside of newsrooms). I'd expected to have children while young, but I didn't know how difficult it could be to have them when older. I had no idea, until writing newspaper articles on the subject, that one in seven couples have problems with fertility.

I'm so worried that I might have plunged head first off the fertility cliff that I get in touch with an IVF expert whom I've previously interviewed for work. I'm hoping he might be able to offer me some silver lining or reassurance. Professor Simon Fishel worked with the team who pioneered the birth of Louise Joy Brown, the world's first 'test tube' baby. I find it hard to believe that during his career something that was so experimental and both hailed as a miracle and decried in the media as a sinister step into a brave new world, has become entirely routine, experienced by millions.

He went on to found CARE fertility, but he can't offer me the assurances I'm looking for: he's found no way of reversing the effects of time on fertility. He confirms that conception rates for women over thirty-five are half those aged twenty-five. As if to offer some comfort to me, he points out that men are affected too, and the number of mutations in sperm almost triple between a twenty-year-old and a forty-year-old. I'm not sure what I should take from this: perhaps it's time to date much younger men to try to balance out the downsides of my age?

It feels odd to me how quickly the journey from trying to avoid pregnancy to wondering if it's even possible comes around. At school we were taught how to avoid pregnancy using condoms or the Pill (I remember a condom being put on a banana in class, which we all thought was hilarious), but there was no mention of how to tackle fertility problems. The emphasis was on not getting pregnant.

A friend, Phil, who teaches science in a London academy tells me that infertility is now mentioned in biology classes, although it's not given the same weight as contraception − perhaps for practical reasons of trying to prevent students from dropping out of their studies. IVF is simply described as fertilisation outside of the body in a laboratory, which is still a lot more than was mentioned when I was at school. IVF was so new then that people talked about the ethics of 'test tube' babies, rather than treating it as a standard procedure.

Even today, age doesn't get a mention as a factor in declining fertility. It must all feel so abstract: I don't imagine that any fourteen-year-old has experienced years of aching to have a child. The idea of turning twenty felt inconceivably distant to me when I was a teenager, while thirty was unimaginably old.

Now I'm beyond that, and I'm only too aware of the potential difficulties in getting and staying pregnant. My mind is whirring as I consider my choices.

Either I wait to meet a partner because love is really important to me − and I've been lucky to have some cartwheeling-amazing relationships as well as some disappointing ones − or I go ahead on my own and try to become a solo parent.

Becoming a solo parent is not my fairy-tale wish. I don't doubt that the ideal way for a child to grow up is with two loving parents. The make-up of traditional families makes sense for both adults and children. But if I choose to wait for love, I also have to feel comfortable with the idea that, by that point, having children might mean joining adoption lists, with years of agonising hope and no guarantee of success. And I don't think I'd have wanted to find out my fertility levels if I had no intention of acting on them.

I know that some women, at this stage, might have chosen to panic-date. Not with any cynicism, but simply finding someone who wants a similar lifestyle and going for it very quickly indeed. And I don't doubt that I could have speedily found someone to have children with. But if they weren't someone I'd consider if I didn't appear to have a fertility deadline looming, I wasn't convinced that we'd last out together. And while one swift divorce might be regarded as a misfortune, two is careless.

When I consider it, it doesn't feel like a choice for me. I could contemplate the idea that I might try my hardest and still not be able to have children (or so I tell myself), but to not even try feels unimaginable, like I'd be sitting on the sidelines watching chances pass me by.

When I arrive home, I book an appointment at a clinic in London, the first they have free, for a week's time, to get a second opinion on my fertility and the options available to me. I tell the consultant that I had been advised by the first clinic to try IVF straight away, which involves harvesting eggs, rather than the less intrusive IUI (artificial insemination). IVF involves being pumped full of hormones to encourage many eggs to grow, then these eggs are collected during surgery before being fertilised in a petri dish. IUI, on the other hand, involves a few scans to check your most fertile time of the month, one hormone injection to trigger ovulation and a pipette of sperm inserted into your vagina. It's one step up from a turkey baster.

'A few months isn't going to make a difference,' the consultant reassures me. 'I wouldn't wait a year to move on to IVF, but if you'd like to give IUI a go first, then you will not lose anything. I would recommend you give it two or three rounds of IUI, and then move straight onto IVF.'

The success rate of artificial insemination is much lower than IVF: it is more comparable with having sex at the perfect moment, and works immediately only about 10 per cent of the time. In comparison, IVF success rates are somewhere between 12 per cent and 58 per cent per cycle, depending on age. But it's still a lottery.

The consultant suggests that if IUI is going to work for me, it would probably be within the first few months. Continuing after that would probably be in vain, but then I have the option to move on to IVF. She says that if that doesn't work, she also has patients who use egg donation, which instinctively feels like a bigger leap without a partner.

I speak to her colleague, Dr Yau Thum, who works at the frontiers of fertility and is currently involved in a research project to give women uterine transplants, allowing those who would otherwise never be able to carry a child to become pregnant. It's important work that will hopefully reduce heartache. I feel like he's giving me a glimpse into the future: by transplanting a uterus, a transgender woman, or a man, could choose to get pregnant and carry a child.

I ask him whether women are experiencing more fertility problems in the twenty-first century, or whether that's simply my perception because I'm at an age when fertility is something that I can no longer take for granted. He suggests that modern lifestyles could be partly responsible: many women focus on their careers in their twenties and early thirties, when their fertility is at its peak, and only think of having children in their late thirties. Some will inevitably face fertility issues, especially if their egg reserve is low, if they have problems such as blocked oviducts (which transport the eggs to the uterus) or have suffered from sexually transmitted diseases.

I've never identified with media depictions of career women who forget about partners and families until it's too late. I'm not enough of a high-flyer and spend swathes of my time thinking about men and children. But Dr Thum's words do make me think how much I'm influenced by both lifestyle and the people around me. I suspect that if everyone I knew had had children in their twenties, I would have felt the pressure sooner. Instead, I only have one friend in my generation who had a child before she was thirty.

Men are also experiencing a decline in fertility, he says, with sperm that aren't mobile: pollution, drugs and unhealthy food are having a major effect.

We chat about how fertility treatment is also more available now. Just a few decades ago, if you couldn't have children, you had to come to terms with it. Many people didn't know that there were alternatives, and those available were talked about in hushed tones.

Talking to Dr Thum helps me realise just how hard it is to experience problems with fertility, and how it affects people's confidence. Patients often feel that they're not good enough or are a failure, and it's common to suffer from depression.

He tells me about a study that suggests if you break the news to a couple that they are infertile, the sadness and pressure that they feel is equal, or sometimes more, than if you tell a patient that they have cancer. Because my dad died of cancer, I find this quite extreme, but he explains that with a cancer diagnosis the person will ask about treatment and prognosis, whereas if they're told they can't be helped with their fertility, there is no more hope; it's a closed door.

I ask him about his experiences of single women using a donor, and he says that there is a level of pressure and responsibility on single people that couples don't feel. He finds that women embarking on a journey to try to become a solo mum will have put a huge amount of thought not only into having a baby but also into how to look after them as they grow up, what they'll do about work and how they'll afford to give them what they need. They'll plan, and test their thinking extensively, even before they pick up the phone to a clinic. This rings true to me: if I had a partner, I don't think I'd plan as far into the future; I'd feel that between the two of us we'd be able to take care of a child with no problems. The chances of two people being made redundant or suffering from ill health are just so much slimmer. With one person, all these possibilities have to be taken into account before trying to conceive.

My consultant gives me an excellent piece of advice: if I am going to embark on fertility treatment, it is important to think positively. 'I tell my patients to stand in front of the mirror and to imagine their body pregnant,' she says, 'To believe this is going to happen.' It's the tiniest glimpse into the lives of many patients who return again and again, each month bringing new disappointment, hoping beyond hope that this time their bodies would carry a baby.

3

Going on a Sperm Hunt

If life were a film, a convenient male best friend would emerge at this point with an offer of sperm and support. In my reality, I look into sperm donation and artificial insemination.

It crosses my mind to ask the hospital to double-check my anti-müllerian hormone levels. On one level, I am so disbelieving of the results that I wonder whether they're inaccurate – whether the clinic had got my results mixed up with someone else's. But that is madness. As a blood test, it gives an accurate result, and clinics rarely make mistakes with people's details. Oddly, I hold on to the shadow of doubt in my mind that perhaps there was a mistake in processing. I'd seen those follicles: wouldn't I be down to one each side if my fertility had dropped so low?

Something stops me from getting another test done. I suspect the rational side of my brain knows that the chances of a results mix-up are so slight that they are negligible, and perhaps, deep down, I know that if I have another test done and it confirms the results of the first test, I won't have that sliver of doubt to hold on to. Also, I've grown attached to the idea of trying to have a baby now. I've considered all the options, and I am ready. Even discarding the hormone test, I know it could be a long, emotional journey. My best chance of having a baby is to act swiftly.

I've never had fairy-tale dreams about white weddings, but I have imagined having children with someone whom I love. Harder than anything, though, is the thought of missing out on children because I am waiting for the perfect partner. Perhaps the results of the fertility tests are starting to sink in.

In the two years since my miscarriage, I no longer seem able to truly enjoy the sweetness of having no responsibilities – I'd been so happy to trade in my freedom for parenthood when I found out I was pregnant.

Weeks after miscarrying, when I was feeling bruised by the world, I remember sitting on the steps outside my flat with a friend, feeling the September morning sun on my face and watching the neighbours load their children into cars to take them off to Saturday morning activities: music lessons, swimming classes, maybe even extra schooling for the unlucky among them.

'I'm so glad my weekends aren't spent doing that,' my friend commented. Perhaps she thought it would be of some comfort to me. Or perhaps it was simply an observation.

I was silent. That's exactly what I'd signed up for in pregnancy. I'd have swapped all the Saturday mornings in the world to bring up my child.

Although time has passed, that ache to be a parent hasn't lessened. My family are supportive, although cautious that I might find the whole experience emotional – and that it could lead to a lot of upset. I think they are especially concerned that I have no partner to support me through it, although at least they know that I wouldn't have to go through the trauma of someone leaving straight after a miscarriage. I'm not in a position where I can lean on someone just for them to remove that support – and for me to then fall flat on my face. And I don't know whether I might have a series of miscarriages ahead that would put a huge strain on any relationship, so perhaps there are some upsides to finding out alone.

The clinic gives me the name of a US sperm bank they recommend. I have no idea what I'll find when I search for it online and have my first exposure to an industry that, estimates suggest, will be worth £5bn in 2025 – and it surprises me. The closest thing the sperm bank resembles is a dating website, only with no flirting and a lot more baby pictures.

Each donor offers a selection of photos of themselves, including as a baby and as an adult. They share information about why they have chosen to become a donor, and provide a little essay about their outlook on life. One of the donors has written a letter to their unborn child: it is moving and full of good advice. When I check, I find out that his sperm is all sold out, and I suspect it is his words rather than the dimples in his cheeks that meant women had ordered vials of his semen, knowing they could pass this letter on to any child.

There is also a huge amount of health information, and this seems to me the most important thing to base my choice of a sperm donor on. The first thing I realise is that everyone has some kind of health issue in their families, whether it's an auntie who died young of breast cancer or a grandfather who had an untimely heart attack. I can't find a cancer-free family, although I do look. But a sprinkling of unlucky health problems, combined with a lot of long life, seem like the most anyone can hope for.

It crosses my mind how strange this is: I can't imagine being in a relationship with anyone and checking up on the health of their uncle, unless it's because I've got to know them and they're sick – certainly not in a hereditary-disease-type way. And I'd feel a bit taken aback if someone's third date chat mentioned family history, allergies and childhood disease. But when you don't know the person, it seems like a good guide.

I also really like that people are asked for their impression of their own character, and to note where they sit on various axes including athletic to couch potato, optimistic to pessimistic, extrovert to introvert, leader to follower and easy-going to controlling. Here, I suspect it's rather like a dating site, and very few people are going to describe themselves as a pessimistic, controlling, non-artistic couch potato – but it's reassuring at least that people believe they are full of good qualities. I find that my shortlist is made up of people who are handsome as well as healthy.

My Milanese flatmate finds the whole thing intriguing and loves looking through the profiles with me. In Roman Catholic Italy, a single person choosing to try to get pregnant by a sperm donor would be breaking the law, so the whole thing is alien to her – and utterly fascinating.

It's incredible that sperm, egg and embryo donation varies so much by country. Whereas the law changed in the UK in 2005, ending donor anonymity, in France sperm and egg donations are absolutely anonymous, and sharing any identifying information about the donor or recipient can be punished by a fine of up to €30,000 or imprisonment of two years.

Non-identifying information is standard from UK clinics, whereas at US- and Danish-based sperm banks a large amount of information – including baby and adult photos – is given to intended parents. Greece, South Africa, Ukraine and Russia also provide more information on the provider of donor sperm than many UK clinics, whereas most European countries give much less information: in Spain and the Czech Republic many clinics will provide only an age and blood group. In these countries, many egg donors and intended parents are matched by the clinics themselves, rather than giving any choice to those undergoing treatment to try to become a parent.

The cost of treatment itself drives many people abroad, often to the Czech Republic and Spain, where a round of IVF costs roughly half the price of the UK. Babies conceived abroad aren't counted in the official UK records, kept by the Human Fertilisation and Embryology Authority, of how many people are having babies conceived with donor sperm or eggs. This means that numbers are always misleading. Nor, of course, are these figures on more informal donor relationships where a clinic isn't used.

I find that looking through an online catalogue really brings the reality of what I am doing home: sperm is not something that has ever featured on my shopping list before. While it's fascinating, having lots of sex to try to conceive would be a lot more fun.

But I duly place my order for three vials of sperm – enough for two rounds of insemination (with a vial spare in case one isn't up to standard, which the clinic recommends doing) and I let the clinic know. Once it arrives from America, they will keep it on ice until I am ready to use it.

I feel grateful for the freedom that women have today, and I know how lucky I am to be born at this time in history. Fifty years ago, a single woman not in love but in want of a child would have had to compromise and pick a man in haste to start courting.

While I was researching donors, I was surprised to learn that it isn't a modern phenomenon, and that donor children have existed for hundreds of years. Henry IV, King of Castile, who reigned between 1425 and 1474, was rumoured to have resorted to artificial insemination so that his wife Princess Juana could have an heir. After six years of marriage, the royal couple's daughter Joanna was born. The King, nicknamed Henry the Impotent, became the subject of court gossip, as people speculated over whether a donor was his daughter's biological father.

Then, in the 1770s, came the first account of artificial insemination from Scottish-born surgeon John Hunter. According to research by Belgian researcher William Ombelet, who has written academic studies on the subject, Hunter advised a cloth merchant who was suffering from severe hypospadias (a condition where the opening usually found at the tip of the penis is on the underside instead) to collect semen, which escaped during sex, in a warmed syringe and then inject it into his partner's vagina.

Officially though, sperm donation in the UK started in the late 1940s, when Dr Mary Barton set up a fertility clinic in London and used sperm donors who biologically fathered hundreds of children, later described as 'Barton's Brood'.

There are now adults in their seventies across Britain who were born to couples where the man was infertile – not to single women, that would have been scandalous at the time – although some of those children were raised by their mothers if the relationship later ended in separation.

Quality sperm donors were limited, and it's been suggested that Barton's husband, Bertold Wiesner, might be the biological father of many hundreds of children.

Before she died, Mary Barton destroyed all the records of the donors she worked with. She would have had no idea that genetic testing was going to mean true anonymity would become a thing of the past in those donor children's lifetimes. Some of the adults she helped to create with donor sperm have found out the identity of their donors and met up with a handful of their hundreds of half-brothers and sisters. But the vast majority have no idea that they weren't conceived by their parents and that their dad is not a biological relative.

Even just a few decades ago, society was more judgemental and less understanding, and Mary Barton's work was shrouded in secrecy.

The more I learn, the more grateful I feel for being born at a time where there's freedom and comparative openness. Parents in the UK aren't legally obliged to be honest with their children about their conception, but it is strongly recommended by donor conception charities and counsellors at fertility clinics.

Nowadays, hiding a child's origins from them is frowned upon by people who work with families with donor children, and the clinic advises me to talk openly to any future child about their origins. I have counselling sessions, both through the clinic and independently, which confirm to me how important it is to be open with any child about how loved they are, and how they are so wanted that I picked a donor to help me bring them into the world.

The clinic counsellor I speak to asks whether I would talk to any future child about their conception and I reply, explaining that it isn't a secret. I'm not ashamed, so I won't be keeping it hidden – instead I am proud to be choosing to try to become a parent.

We talk about the choice I am making, and the counsellor advises me that it's best to introduce the topic, in child's language, from a young age. And she does mean really young, from when a child is first speaking – usually around two years old, depending on the development of the child – so there are never any surprises.

She explains that, under British law, any future children I have would be able to get in touch with their biological father at eighteen, and any half-siblings (if both children want to) when they both reach eighteen. It's important to refer to the biological father as a donor, so that it does not set a child up with any false hopes that the donor will swoop in during adulthood as a daddy.

It's really important to me to know where I come from and my history: it has helped to shape my identity and, more importantly, give me a sense of belonging. It helps me to understand that while we're only around for a tiny burst of time, those who come before us live on in us, and hopefully – if we don't mess up the world irreparably – those who live after will carry a little of us into the future. I imagine many children might feel similarly. I'm delighted that Britain changed the law in 2005 to offer this right to children conceived by sperm donors. They can now satisfy their curiosity as to where their long fingers or their love of sport might have come from.

Sadly, this now means that fewer men are happy to donate sperm, worried perhaps about some sort of responsibility in later life, or just worried that a decision made on a whim will come back to haunt them decades later. Consequently, sperm banks are running low, and many women end up looking abroad for donors. But this is still better, I feel, than not offering the children the option of understanding their origins.

When I was growing up, I wondered if I could have been adopted and if there was a possibility that I was descended from royalty or famous actors, even though really I knew I wasn't. Perhaps there is a genre of children's books that feature adopted heroines. But if I really had no way of knowing anything about one of my biological parents, I think I'd have created such a fantastic father figure that no reality could live up to it. For children who share a similar type of imagination (and I'm happy to acknowledge that this might have made me a slightly odd child), the lack of anonymity is a wonderful, grounding thing.

Depending on their personality, they could otherwise spend a lifetime wondering if every man that looks similar to them could possibly be related.

I'm looking forward to our culture becoming more open. In sixty years we've seen homosexuality go from being illegal to being, for the most part, celebrated, and I have no doubt that our acceptance of different shapes and sizes of family will follow a similar trajectory. Once we blow away the final taboos over donation, fertility and concepts of family, men will not feel that they need to shy away from sperm donation – and women won't need to go abroad.

* * *

My menstrual cycle starts to be medicalised. I have scans to see if eggs are growing, and to monitor the follicles from which an egg is likely to be released that month. Women start puberty with around 400,000 follicles, each with the potential to release an egg, or ovum. Midway through each menstrual cycle one enlarges – becoming dominant – preparing to release an egg when a woman ovulates. I find it odd thinking about how much is going on biologically to mean that we can create babies, just as I find it a little peculiar to think of blood being pumped around my veins, of 300 billion new cells being produced every day and my brain turning down the volume if I raise my voice so that I don't deafen myself, while I'm oblivious to this incredible machine that means I'm here.

I'm working three days a week in an office, so as much as possible I try to arrange fertility appointments outside these days, and I start occasionally slipping off to the 'doctor' or 'dentist' whenever this isn't possible.

If anyone at work is keeping a close eye on my movements, and my general distractedness from all things non-pregnancy related, they'll have concluded that I am going for lots of job interviews. As it is, I think they're oblivious. I frequently spend my time in the office chatting about how much I love my nephews, the sea and my campervan.

Timing is everything: when my egg is ripe I'm to give myself a hormone injection to trigger ovulation. I don't mind being scanned – someone looking at my ovaries and telling me they are doing their job feels somehow reassuring.

It's a private clinic. I don't qualify for NHS support as a single person unless I've been struggling to get pregnant for a long time – which shows me that society hasn't yet accepted solo parents. It is only if a single woman has been through twelve rounds of IUI, which would cost around £20,000 including donor sperm, that she would qualify for infertility treatment paid for by the National Health Service.

It does cross my mind to pretend to my doctor that I am in a lesbian relationship in order to qualify for free treatment (if I pretend to be in a straight relationship, I think there would have been some questions about why I am sourcing sperm elsewhere). But I feel that this could easily go wrong. I'm not a good enough actress, and what if a doctor ends up suggesting my friend carries a baby instead? Therefore, although my doctor offers support, and sends me for as many blood tests as the NHS will offer, there is little more that she can do.

This doesn't mean that solo mums are a wealthy crowd: the drive to have a child is so strong that they share resourcefulness over riches. I've met solo mums who are canny with credit cards, swapping so that they never pay interest on the debt they've accrued, and others who've remortgaged homes on the chance of becoming a parent. But these do rely on being able to get credit, or having property to borrow against, and I think it's very difficult indeed to embark on fertility treatment as a single woman if you're not financially stable. Some women adopt a do-it-yourself approach and look online for men offering their sperm for free.

My trips to the clinic are regular, because my ovaries are monitored every couple of days as I approach ovulation. Each time, I sip a cup of hot chocolate in the waiting room, telling myself this wouldn't be on offer on the NHS (although I would have happily traded in my hot chocolate for free treatment), while listening out for my name to be called.

I'm not comfortable with taking medication when I don't feel unwell, and I find the idea of the trigger injection, which causes ovulation, unsettling. I say to one nurse at the fertility clinic that I will maybe not inject, and just rely on nature to take its course and for the sperm to be inseminated.

'You could do that,' she tells me. 'But this makes sure you ovulate, and you don't want to take any chances. If it were me, I'd be having the injection.' Her words of encouragement are all that I need.

I am so baffled when I pick up the package containing the needle and ovulation fluid that the pharmacist helps me out, and makes sure I've got the right place in my tummy, below my belly button and off to one side, before injecting it for me. It isn't painful.

My body is ready. The sperm is taken off ice, and inseminated. I've been told to expect it to be almost pain-free, just a moment of discomfort similar to a smear test. This is not my experience. I am nervous and can't relax; I feel like my insides are being grazed as a doctor puts a catheter inside me through which she'll insert the liquid carrying sperm. I keep thinking of women in the early twentieth century who'd lain back and thought of England – surely they weren't having as bad a time as this? Then, after all the poking and prodding (have I mentioned already that sex is a million times nicer?) I have to wait a fortnight to see if I am pregnant. A very long fortnight.

4

The Idolisation of Motherhood

I can't think of anything over those two weeks other than whether I'm going to have the chance of becoming a parent or not. And I start to wonder why it is so important to me – and want to feel reassured, in case it's just not possible, that parenthood is not always as fulfilling as it might seem from snapshots of friends' lives. It seems strange to me that as an independent woman with a good career I'd never considered not having children.

I think my obvious adoration of my two nephews, William and Dylan, means that all my friends presumed that I would want to have my own children at some point. And I've never seen my brother and sister-in-law so brimming with happiness as when their sons were born.

But it stems from much earlier than that. It was just always a given for me. When I was six or seven, I preferred clambering around in trees and reading to playing with dolls, but this wasn't a rejection of being a mother any more than my wish for an à la carte kitchen was an early sign of a future as a cordon bleu chef.

In secondary school, aged around twelve, I remember saying to friends that I'd have the first of my two children (a girl and boy) in my mid-twenties. I wanted to do exactly as my mum had done when it came to having children. Little did I know quite how unusual it would be for someone living in London to get pregnant before thirty and take five years off work to look after children by the time I grew up and became an adult. (I'm not sure that London, with its Peter Pan culture and emphasis on careers above families, has got things right: there's a reason why there are so many fertility clinics in this city.)

I feel that the default life is to follow in the footsteps of parents, and perhaps that's part of the societal expectation of having children. But then, I also thought I'd work as a barrister and own an Old English sheepdog, neither of which my parents did – and, as it turns out, nor have I, so far.

I have been open with close friends and my family about hoping to become pregnant, and I am overwhelmed by the love I feel from those who have told me that they think I'd make a good parent, and who offered to help out if they could.

Some of the most supportive words come from my mum. 'You do know that I'll love you just as much if you don't have children?' she says. I cry. I know that having children is something incredibly important to her, and perhaps that has rubbed off on me. I don't think, when I was younger, that she'd considered a possible world where I wouldn't have children either.

I know what an important role being a grandparent is to her and the pleasure it gives her, just as being an auntie is a great joy to me. I think I feel that I've somehow let her down, or am lesser, by not having had children of my own. I really appreciate her relieving me from the pressures that I have inflicted upon myself.

I've felt my ovaries crying out, just as many women have, I'm sure, but it was cultural pressure as much evolutionary desire that I experienced. Society is more accepting, currently, of a woman who wishes that she can have a child but is unable to, than someone who simply chooses a different path. Female politicians and people in the public eye feel the need to explain away a lack of children.

A family friend, after a funeral and long whisky-fuelled wake, told me how angry she felt at the pressures on women to have babies. She had her son, who is now a teenager, when she was young and thinks that if it weren't for societal pressures few people would otherwise sacrifice so much for children. I was furious with her for not acknowledging all the women who don't feel the pressure until it's late, and then they would do almost anything to experience the motherhood that she so takes for granted.

I've seen friends who were adamant that they didn't want children at thirty become pregnant a few years later, and I have observed single friends feel slightly awkward over the issue of fertility and its rapid disappearance around forty because they're aware that it might put unnecessary pressure on any new relationships.

Of those who have taken a look at what motherhood entailed and thought, 'Lovely, but not for me', I know only one who's out and proud. And she spent her childhood bringing up her brothers, so she feels that she's already done it once over.

I've heard people talk about the lack of status of being a mother, compared to when they're at (official) work, and describe it as twenty-four-hour unacknowledged toil. This might be true within their families, if they feel that they have a partner who doesn't appreciate the sheer hard work that goes into parenting, but it seems to me that being a mother in society is the opposite: it's an exalted role. Society decrees time and again that it's the most important job in the world. And it's perhaps for this reason that there's bravery in rejecting it.

I want to hear from women who look at the world through different lenses to me to reassure me that if I can't get pregnant I'm still going to have a fulfilling life – one that others choose. I want to feel that I won't be second best if I can't have children.

Because I know so few people who have openly decided not to become parents, I speak to a friend of a friend about her choice not to become a mother. Deciding not to become a mother when in a stable relationship feels like the complete inverse of my situation. But we've both raised an accidental challenge to conventional society. And it takes courage to follow your own wishes if they don't follow the standard train tracks that we ride along through life, often without realising.

Rachel lives close to me, and we meet in a south-east London pub one evening, too early for it to be busy. My first impression of her is of someone confident and independent (she met her husband six years ago in a pub, where she chatted him up).

She is in her mid-thirties, married, and works as a lawyer in a City bank. In our society, her standard next move would be to have children. But she says that she just doesn't feel that biological drive that she knows some of her friends have experienced. It isn't that she woke up one morning and decided 'children aren't for me', but more that every time a milestone has come up in her life where she's questioned whether she wants to try to become a parent, she's thought: *not really.*

When she and her husband first fell in love, there were

times when he asked whether she wanted kids, and she did reply saying 'maybe'. When he asked whether she'd want them with him, she said that if she were to have kids it would be with him. But subsequently, she's realised that this was probably more pillow talk than truthful – and when she said 'maybe', she really meant 'no'.

She says she hasn't given as much thought to his feelings on the issue as he probably deserves, but the reality is that she's the one who would have to give birth and would be doing a lot of the heavy lifting.

'He's ambivalent, which means I'd absolutely not want to: you can't have two ambivalent people,' she explains. 'I can't even commit to a pet.'

If she went ahead with having children, it would be because of expectation, rather than from choice. She thinks that if she's not 100 per cent committed to the idea, it would be unfair on the child (who she's very aware is likely to want support beyond the age of eighteen). And she's unsure how she'd handle bringing up a child, or children, on her own if she and her partner don't stay together. She's very honest and aware that a huge amount of her second-guessing is about fears of things that might not happen. But her logic is faultless: so much so that it makes me wonder whether that's the reason for the existence of such a strong biological drive, because it overrides any logical weighing up of whether or not to have children. I'm yet to meet someone who's had children for logical reasons rather than emotional ones. The closest I've heard is people who decide to start a family in case they regret not doing so in later life, but this is to counter a future emotional loss.

Rachel's aware that motherhood has been put on a pedestal and feels that there's pressure to do it in an obsessive, interactive, hands-on way. And if you don't, then you're doing it poorly. But this is impossible if you maintain your job. She feels that the only reason careers and motherhood are incompatible is because of the current inflexibility of careers. 'There's pressure on and resentment towards mothers who aren't in the workforce fully, and to those who are in the workforce and aren't committing themselves fully to motherhood. So women can't win, right?'

Her parents were never married, but were together for eighteen years, although they split up for part of that. But she doesn't think their relationship put her off being a parent.

Unlike my friendship groups, where most of my friends now have children, Rachel says that more than half of her friends don't, and many of those who do waited until their forties. Some of her friends wouldn't do it over again even though they love their children. They've found it harder than they thought and are mourning the loss of their lives.

The only pressure she's ever felt has been from her mum, who gave a speech at her wedding, got a bit weepy and blurted out: 'Have a baby.' Rachel was furious: she'd been hoping to hear a few words about her husband and her. But the rest of her family has been very relaxed about her not having a child, saying that if she and her husband had a child, that kid would be cool, but that there are enough cool kids in the world. Aside from the one blip from her mother, she feels no procreation pressure whatsoever.

It makes me wonder about the pressure I feel to have children: is it really social pressure, or is it more a longing stemming from me? If I don't want something, I think I'm confident enough to reject it or ignore it rather than being swayed by social pressure.

But she does think that women should be able to become mothers and not fear that it's a tsunami that will wash away everything they hold dear and totally change their identity.

This isn't a fear I share; the trade-in of nights out for bringing up a child is something that doesn't give me any concern, although I completely understand how valid it is. I just hope that one day I'll be in want of a babysitter.

Although Rachel appears to have made her decision lightly, almost unaware that she is bucking convention, I admire her for holding true to her dreams. I begin to understand what a huge difference the people you're sur-rounded by make to your sense of normality: if many of your friends have chosen not to become parents, there aren't constant questions and expectations about children when-ever you are in a serious relationship. But I realise also that I'm a pedlar of these conventions and see the world through family-tinted lenses. When I see a pal with a rounded belly, I presume pregnancy rather than pizza; if someone's not drinking, I always jump to conclusions. I'd never say a word, but I do mentally add on seven months to work out their rough due date.

I'm reassured by chatting to Rachel that, for many people, it's a logical decision not to have children. I also want to ask the opinion of those women who I have huge respect for who have become mothers and dare to say that they regret it. This, to me, goes against every cultural expectation there is and breaks so many societal conventions that I imagine it's a room-silencing confession.

I hope different perspectives on parenthood will help me if I get news that children aren't going to be possible for me. If I can find one tiny bit of me that doesn't feel disappointed if I get the news I'm dreading, I'm sure that will grow and, eventually, in years to come, I'll find it in me to believe it's worked out for the best. But I need to find that tiny bit first.

I speak to Louisa, thirty-six, a stay-at-home mum, who is

someone who regrets becoming a mum. She's married and her daughter is now a year and a half old. When she was growing up she did a lot of babysitting, and although she didn't particularly like it, she was really good with children, and they loved playing with her. Despite people telling her how great she'd be as a parent, she went through most of her life not wanting children. She wasn't really geared up for marriage either, hoping instead to be single, or perhaps have a long-term boyfriend. Her dream life included a great career, a penthouse flat and two Tonkinese cats.

Her childhood was tough, and she spent years in counselling to deal with the depression and anxiety she suffered as a result. As she worked towards becoming stronger and improving her self-esteem, she rejected lots of things that she considered were unhealthy beliefs. Heaped in with this was her preference for being single over relationships, and over not wishing to become a mum. She thought these were natural things that everyone wanted, and it was simply her unhealthy thinking making her believe that she didn't want them.

Her expectations of motherhood were that it would almost be something self-improving, and would help her to become a more rounded person.

Louisa thought that her husband – whom she truly loves – and she would create a beautiful child who would nap next to them and be an angelic creature to enhance their lives. It didn't cross her mind that her future child would be just another child, like the ones that used to annoy her when she babysat all those years ago. She expected it to be hard work but ultimately rewarding. But she's found that it's not. It's a good reminder to me that everyone's experience of motherhood is different – and how easy I find it to romanticise parenthood.

When Louisa learnt that she was pregnant, she was happy for a day or two, and then she started to think that it was a bad idea. She mentioned abortion to her husband but knew it would break his heart. But as the weeks passed, she found that she enjoyed pregnancy and didn't really think about the reality that this was only the beginning.

She imagined motherhood as a montage of precious moments: pushing a stroller with a coffee in hand, cuddles with a sweet little baby while an artfully placed tear of happiness rolled down her cheek.

She loves her daughter very much, but it's as far from her Hollywood montage as it could be. She says she has never felt anything magical about being a parent. Instead, she feels trapped in a never-ending babysitting job that she can't quit. She describes the relentlessness so vividly that I do have to pinch myself and check that I'm not basing my quest to be a mother on a fairy tale, albeit one rewritten for the twenty-first century.

When her daughter was four weeks old, Louisa realised the reality, which she found to be a lot of hard work with little reward. She knew that she had a very difficult baby who wouldn't sleep, but by the time her daughter was seven or eight months old she was a lot more settled. Louisa's feelings didn't improve, however, and she felt as if the truth was crashing down around her: she disliked kids. She didn't even care that her daughter had become an 'easy' baby, she just didn't want to go down this path at all. She didn't even want an additional person in her house and felt that she was an introvert who was now signed up for a lifelong roommate when she'd always just wanted to live alone.

If she had a choice, she wouldn't want to spend her time having play dates for her daughter or watching *Sesame Street*; she wants to be an adult and only do adult things. But she is ashamed of feeling this way.

Louisa believes her marriage has been ruined by having her daughter, because she has been so stressed and unhappy since her daughter became part of their lives. Although she loves her daughter hugely, before she was in the world Louisa and her husband had a lot of fun. Now, she says, they've lost each other. He spends a lot of time trying to carve out breaks for her; she feels guilty that he's creating situations that give her the respite she needs to survive. The couple have lost lots of friends, as well as losing their freedom to go travelling.

While she feels resentful of the situation, she doesn't feel resentful towards her daughter, who she says is a completely innocent party. And she hopes very much that her daughter doesn't know how she feels. Instead, Louisa feels resentful towards her partner every single day. Despite loving him, she wishes she had never met him. 'He's wonderful, but it was a ghastly mistake,' she says. She believes society duped her into believing that a husband and kids was the right thing to do.

If she were able to go back in time, Louisa would neither marry nor have children, and instead would pursue a career that she could excel at and provide for herself. There'd be no man involved. But if she tells people about her feelings, they don't want to know. Even when she goes to talk to her doctor about her mental health, he doesn't want to hear negativity about motherhood. It has opened her eyes to gender inequality, how the world expects women to give up everything for their offspring, and she's become a feminist as a result. When she confides in her friends and family, they too don't seem to want to hear what she's saying and will frequently try to convince her that she doesn't feel that way. As a result, Louisa feels very alone.

I find it hard hearing about Louisa's life and feel sad for both her and her daughter. It must feel so isolating for Louisa to experience parenthood and find it underwhelming, while films, books, culture, friends and family depict it as being the opposite. I wonder if she feels that there's some mass deception going on, and she's the only who feels like she's being honest enough to speak up.

She reminds me that it's impossible to predict how I will experience motherhood: I don't question my resolve to have a baby, but I do remind myself that when I'm with my nephews it's chaotic, real, wonderful and exhausting – and nothing like a Hollywood film. It reassures me that I'm not trying to create a fantasy family where there are no tears, only cuddles.

For me, acknowledging regret in becoming a mother feels almost like the ultimate taboo – and a far, far harder thing to voice than my wish to become a mother so much that I would happily do it alone. I suspect this is why so few women talk about it. But I have no doubt that there are others who suffer secretly, afraid to say the unthinkable, watching other mothers in parks and play clubs while wondering if they're the only ones who'd rather be living a different life. I only hope that I am lucky enough to become one of those parents in parks and play clubs. Becoming a parent feels so long awaited that I can't imagine feeling anything other than grateful, though I know that, in reality, parenting has its tough moments – especially with no support from a partner.

I find this spectrum of motherhood fascinating, and want to know more. I get in touch with the professor of sociology at Oxford Brookes University, Tina Miller, who has studied parenthood throughout her career, as well as being a mother to three now-adult daughters. She agrees that it can be incredibly brave to speak out about regrets. She is currently undertaking her second study on motherhood, a generation after she did the first.

I ask her about the idolisation of motherhood, the way that it seems to be an exalted role, but one that frequently defines women. She says that the role of a mother is what society wants it to be, and that shifts through history. It wasn't always idolised in the same way, but after the Second World War, when people wanted women to be back in their homes after they had been out at work supporting the war effort, there was a sudden surge of interest in the theory of bonding and development of attachment. This work helped to shift the role of women by emphasising the importance of the mother in the home, positioning them as the primary carer and homemaker. It was very successful: women started getting blamed if correct attachment hadn't taken place. This was a shift in the mother–child relationship from the previous seen-and-not-heard child role. Our society is now becoming increasingly child-centric, with the needs of babies and children elevated and those of the parents becoming secondary.

Expectations on mothers are increasing and intensifying. In her current research, where she interviews mothers before and after they've had their babies, Professor Miller's noticing more societal pressure for intensive parenting, with a focus on producing a successful individual. This can involve the child becoming a 'project', she says. I've seen how many extracurricular activities friends' children take part in, with swimming and dancing and trampolining, and she says that this rise is dramatic. Canadian academic, Annette Lareau, describes this as 'concerted cultivation of children' and has found it is a very middle-class thing.

This adds extra pressure on women, especially because within many households both parents (if there are two parents) are at work. I wonder how this will affect me if I'm able to become a parent: will I feel double the pressure because of parenting alone?

Professor Miller says that she'd like women to feel that they have permission to relax and ignore this trend of more intensified and competitive parenting, and spend a few more boring afternoons at home where children decide what to do. But she recognises that this is hard when mothering is under surveillance – often by other women. 'It's hard to say to other mums at the school gate that actually you don't do any of the activities everyone else is talking about,' she warns me. I can imagine how easy it is to fall into the trap of feeling that a child will miss out if they haven't explored baby sensory or baby rhyme time, or, when they're older, French club or karate, or any of the hundreds of things on offer. And I suspect that I'll feel especially scrutinised by others because I don't have a partner. I imagine that I'd find it very easy to try to be a perfect parent, and trying to show that I can offer as much as a mother and father put together.

Overall, Professor Miller thinks it's a 'blooming difficult' time to be a parent, and guilt – which every mother feels – plays a big role in that. No one is immune, and quite often it starts even before a baby comes into this world, or during, with birth leaving some women feeling that they haven't done well. Guilt forms a Holy Trinity of emotions alongside its running mates: worry and stress. Worry is often linked to the idea of having control and a sense of getting things right, whereas in reality there are so many ways to be a mother. This sense is heightened because all new mothers are doing something completely new, with the highest stakes they've ever experienced: a life to care for. Parents can suddenly feel out of control and completely de-skilled, and many wonder how on earth are they are going to manage all the different demands. I wonder whether these emotions of guilt would be heavier on one pair of shoulders, or whether I'd be so run off my feet as a solo mum that I wouldn't get much space or time for worrying.

On average, women now have their first baby at thirty-two in the UK, and so they are used to having a sense of control over their lives. Perhaps that makes it harder for them when children arrive than if they had never experienced control in the first place.

In our chat, Professor Miller then touches on something that I feel gives me a key to understanding why becoming a mother feels so important to me, beyond the love that I want to give to a child and the desire to watch them grow up and explore their way through the world.

She feels that motherhood is linked ultimately to femininity and essentialism by our society. To be considered a 'real' woman, you're expected to reproduce (even though she says that she wanted to be known as a successful academic, and so did not share with some academic colleagues that she also had children). And I realise that's it. Becoming a mother is so intrinsically bound to my own ideals of being a woman, and of femininity, that of course I've never challenged it. While it feels ingrained in me, it's an understanding of being a woman that many people would dispute and that logically feels so outdated. I feel strongly that women are much more than mothers; that their ability to bring up children has nothing to do with their worth in society, and yet it's something that I seem unable to separate, within myself, from womanhood. After speaking to Rachel and Louisa, and considering other life paths, I am no less convinced that this is the direction I want to follow.

For all the romantic notions contained within motherhood, it's the time I observe many friends' lives become more traditional. They may be successful, ambitious career women with equal partnerships and shared responsibilities for keeping their homes running, but bring in a tiny, dependent baby and, for many, they unconsciously mimic their parents' lives. Sometimes – even in the twenty-first century – 'mother' also means 'housekeeper'. And I've seen how hard that can be. Other friends share things out differently, or employ a nanny who runs their home for them, but the majority of dads I know – all of whom are hands-on and devoted to their children – do not equally split domestic responsibilities with their partners. History is to blame. For me, there'll be no question over reverting to traditional roles: I'll be both carer and provider. The thought of making sure I can look after children and offer them the chances I've had makes me want to be able to invent more time so that I can focus on my career without having to sacrifice being with them.

If I were in a relationship, I'm pretty sure that I'd feel hugely resentful if I were expected to do all the childcare, or be solely responsible for keeping the flat clean. As it is, I'm always a little taken aback when people refer to looking after their children as 'babysitting' – even though it's usually said in a well-meaning way. As it is, if I'm lucky enough to be able to become a solo mum, I'll have to do it all but will have no one to feel resentful towards.

5

Thin Blue Lines

I become so impatient that I do a pregnancy test a week after having sperm inseminated. It comes out positive. For one moment, I feel hopeful as I stare at the two lines on the test. Something doesn't seem quite right, however. I then look online and find that the hormone-trigger injection gives false positives. I'm disappointed but oddly not surprised. It had felt somehow it was too easy. I continue to hope for two lines on the pregnancy test in another week.

My Internet search takes me to forums full of women talking about fertility treatment and sharing wishes for successful treatment. The sign-off 'Baby Dust', to wish luck, is ubiquitous. It's meant so supportively and positively that I'm not sure why I find it slightly cringeworthy. I am intrigued by all these people using acronyms for negative and positive pregnancy tests: BFP for 'big fat positive' and BFN for 'big fat negative', and DPO for 'days post ovulation'. Some of the advice shared feels like false reassurance that people wouldn't believe themselves (a woman who is bleeding at the time of her period probably is just having her period, and the chances are slim that it's spotting from an embryo implanting), but this is interspersed with more practical advice. It offers women a sense of solidarity as they go through repeated cycles of trying to get pregnant. I become a lurker, rather than a poster, reading other people's conversations rather than contributing myself. I find people's experiences really helpful to read about: the information about how long a trigger injection stays in your blood; people's symptoms in the first days of pregnancy. But I feel that fertility treatment is already swallowing up huge swathes of my life, and I feel slightly obsessed by Project Pregnancy already. I don't want to indulge myself by giving over my remaining free time to these forums.

Alongside these forums, some people use social media to support each other through IVF treatment, sharing the month of their cycle so that they can link up with others in a similar situation. I'm not sure how I feel about sharing my cycle with other people: at the end of the month some people will be cautiously celebrating, and others will be going back for another round. I'm not sure whether for me it could add more pressure to an already fraught situation or whether I'd really appreciate the solidarity and encouragement. It concerns me that it would make it feel like success and failure, and that I'm not a big enough person that delight would be my overriding emotion towards others who're successful with the thing that I most want in the world, rather than a sense of 'Why not me?'

These online forum users seem mainly to be women with partners, rather than single women. This scarcity of women in the same situation was noted by a solo mum, Rebecca, when she was trying to become pregnant four years ago.

She didn't know any solo mums, so she sent a message

through the Donor Conception Network, the charity that supports families with donor-conceived children, to see if anyone in her position wanted to meet up for a coffee. After meeting up with a couple of women, she set up a group called Fertility Buddies on social media to help them keep in touch as they tried to get pregnant.

Now, four years later, more than 400 single women share the ups and downs of their fertility journey and confide in people in similar situations – often more honestly than with their friends and family. Rebecca says that there are conversations about rectal pessaries and how stretchy vaginal mucus is before ovulation – a level of detail that people might feel a lot less comfortable sharing with anyone who is not going through the same process. And there is also an outpouring of congratulations when people hear that someone has got pregnant, and love and condolences when women miscarry.

Many of the women in the group have met in real life, and Rebecca organises picnics each year where many strong friendships have formed. She tells me that she loves to follow everyone's journeys: one year a woman came along to the picnic considering whether to try to become a single parent; the next year she had a pregnancy bump and the following year she brought her baby with her.

Rebecca got pregnant almost four years ago from donor sperm using artificial insemination. It took three attempts at insemination, and she found the whole process of going to a fertility clinic to try to conceive felt like an out-of-body experience.

She appreciates the support that women give each other through what can be a very lonely process. With her son about to start school, she's trying to make him a sibling but is struggling with artificial insemination and having to weigh up whether to go through IVF. She says that if it weren't for other solo mums, some of whom are making similar decisions, she would find it isolating.

While I find it heartening to know that there is a group of women in exactly the same situation, all trying to become mothers, I also feel that I need to think of something other than trying to get pregnant. I join the group, but I don't want to spend my time unconsciously scrolling through any online world. But I find it hugely reassuring to know that it's there, in case of emergencies. I suspect this is how many other people feel – it's a place for support if in need. I notice the frequency of people posting about miscarriages; it makes me feel very sad, although it's perhaps reflective that most people making the decision to become a solo mum are slightly older than the average first-time mum.

I retreat from this supportive online world, aware that hopes of motherhood and concerns about my fertility are already consuming huge amounts of my time. I keep doing pregnancy tests, the line getting fainter and fainter as the hormones run out of me until one turns negative. I stare at it for so long, I start believing that I can see a faint line. I do another test and will it to be positive. Only if I stare and stare at the white window, can I make out the faintest line that shows the power of my imagination. Then I get my period.

The next month follows the same pattern: scans, trigger injection, insemination the next day. After the treatment I am told to lie back on the hospital bed for fifteen minutes, and then a nurse will come back and I can go home.

When she comes back, I check whether it would be more effective if I rest for a little longer. Assured that it wouldn't, I set off home.

The month before, I'd got home from the insemination

and spent the evening lying on my sofa, barely speaking to my flatmates, as I felt so busy willing the sperm to do their best. I'd pictured the *Look Who's Talking* opening credits, with sperm tap-tap-tapping at the outside of the egg with one hopefully fertilising it.

This month, Rob, a friend of mine who now lives in New York, is in town and we've planned to go out for dinner. Rob is a signed-up introvert who is proud to keep his friends limited to a dozen. This makes being one of them a hugely flattering experience. I met him when we worked together, many years ago, and every woman in the office had a secret crush on him. He was completely oblivious to our collective admiration.

Since then, he's moved across the Atlantic with his girl-friend, and has spent a long time waiting to get a green card. He spends the evening telling me anecdotes about his more eccentric colleagues, keeping me laughing and distracted. I tell him why I'm not drinking. (Some people do drink after insemination, just as it is quite natural to continue drinking after having unprotected sex, but after going to such great lengths to get pregnant, I don't want to do anything that could be anything other than helpful.) I laugh so much during the evening that I forget that I've just started a fortnight of waiting.

During the following week, I mull over whether I want to push on to a third round of insemination, or if I am wiser to move straight on to IVF.

I even repeat the daftness of doing an early pregnancy test that comes out positive. The next day: negative. I am so despondent about the whole thing. The hormone triggers make my body believe that I am pregnant: my breasts are swollen, my tummy feels bloated, and the sleepiness is almost overwhelming. But it is all a cruel illusion from synthetic hormones. I feel unattractive and hormonal.

After work one night, I go to visit a friend in north

London who has barely slept over the last three months on account of having a baby with colic who feels especially uncomfortable at night. On the way to see her, I suddenly feel faint and weak. So much so that I get off the bus and go to a garage where I buy two bars of chocolate. I eat one very quickly, feeling that I must have very low blood sugar levels and hoping that this will stop me from passing out. I used to experience this faint feeling when I was a child and forgot to have breakfast on a Saturday, and two hours later would feel as if I was about to collapse. Once I've reassured myself that I'm not going to lose consciousness, I call a cab. I arrive, still feeling a little bit shaken. After a couple of hours and dinner with friends, I start feeling a little bit stronger.

I go home and cry, and set out a plan. I decide to move on to IVF treatment, where embryos are formed in petri dishes – at least that way the egg is definitely fertilised. I think the drugs are likely to be an onslaught for my body, and I expect to react sensitively to them, so I am concerned about the impact, but this will give me the very best chance of getting pregnant.

The following day I take another test: positive. The faintest line, barely positive, it could almost be my imagination, again. But it's enough for me to start hoping. Could the faintness I felt have been the embryo implanting, the shift as my body started diverting all its energy away from me and towards the little ball of rapidly splitting cells that could, would, hopefully become a baby?

A week later, and dozens more pregnancy tests, I realise I really, truly am pregnant. I cry with delight. I cry with hormones. I cry with relief.

* * *

I tell my friend Lucinda, and she admits that when she was pregnant she ordered a job lot of fifty pregnancy tests because she wanted to keep checking. She was there for me through my two miscarriages and I think she is as happy and hopeful as I am that I am pregnant again.

I don't dare hope for too much: I've been so hurt before after seeing a heartbeat and then miscarrying, and I want to protect myself from feeling that level of devastation again.

I have music festival tickets for the following week, booked with friends, months before. I remember thinking that it would be a good distraction from the fertility roller coaster. Instead, I feel exhausted. My campervan breaks down, so we all end up camping. The weather stays fine, so I snooze in fields in front of bands and comedy performers over the course of the weekend. It is wonderful in a slow-paced, sun-drenched way. The friends I am with drop me back at my tent by 11pm each night for more rest, and then go out dancing.

When I get back I book an eight-week scan, to check that the little foetus inside me is growing at the expected rate. I take to prodding my breasts to check that they are still aching.

My mum comes with me for the scan. I wait as the Doppler is inserted inside me. The nurse doing the scan pauses, looks, and quickly tells me that there's a heartbeat. She turns the screen around so that I can see. I cry. My mum cries too. I explain that last time I was pregnant I saw a heartbeat, but the foetus wasn't the right size. The nurse says that this little wriggler is the expected size, and that there's no sign for concern. I'm officially pregnant.

I feel lucky simply for getting pregnant so swiftly. Many women becoming solo mums are slightly older than average, and so fertility problems are not unusual. It causes huge amounts of heartache.

* * *

I become more and more tired. The tiny baby growing inside me is depleting all my energy, and I could happily sleep at any point. I feel as if I am peeling myself out of bed in the morning after a heavy night, with a blurry head and dry mouth. Just like with a hangover, I have an increased sensitivity to smell and a decreased tolerance to everything, and everyone, around me.

In the few moments where I feel fully awake, I worry that I am selfish. I've chosen to make a baby who will have one grandparent, while I still have two. It will have no father, and no grandfathers. Luckily, my brother and two nephews will be great role models, and I vow to myself that I'll make sure that my male friends are very involved in this baby's life: I love the men in my life and I don't want my baby to grow up mistrustful or uncomfortable when not surrounded by women.

I rationalise it, reminding myself that although parenting might be selfless, the initial decision to bring a child into the world – if it's a planned pregnancy – is always, on some level, a selfish one. It's not being done for the survival of the human species, or because any individual's genes are so spectacular that they must be captured in future generations, whether the person having a baby is single or with a partner.

Any time I dare to hope that I'll be able to carry my baby for long enough to have a healthy start in life, I quickly start feeling concerned as to whether I'll be a good mum. I know I have a lot of love to give.

Lucinda helps: 'You know, all you have to do is love this baby,' she says. 'Honestly. The rest everyone muddles through and gets wrong and right. As long as he or she knows that you'll be there, that's all that matters.'

I want to learn more about whether this guilt and self-ishness I'm feeling is justified, so I get in touch with Dr Sophie Zadeh, research associate at the Centre for Family Research at Cambridge University, to find out about her research into families. We meet on the South Bank in London, by the Thames, and I'm struck by two things. Firstly, she's probably too young to have ever considered this option for herself. (Certainly, until just a few years ago, I would never have given a moment's thought to the idea that I might not be in an amazing relationship at the point when I'd want children.) Secondly, I think how good she must be at her job: she seems so interested in me that I find myself chatting very openly.

Dr Zadeh started working with families because she's interested in looking at widely held assumptions and whether they're based on reality; for example, people frequently talk about staying together for the kids. She's interested in whether this is based on any truth or a myth.

When she started her work into single mothers whose children are conceived using sperm donors, she expected to find some women who were anti-tradition. Instead, she has found that stories like my own are by far the most common, and solo mums are very ordinary women, even if their path to parenthood is unusual.

In her research, she's found that people are often pro-tradition and anti-tradition within one sentence, saying, for example, 'I'm really pleased I've had this child in this way because it's better than being divorced' and then also 'I wish I were married.' I totally understand this contradiction. I can imagine myself saying both of these things.

While she's found that solo mothers are a diverse group, Dr Zadeh says that one thing they share is that they are all good parents. 'But that's probably true of all parents who use assisted reproduction methods,' she says. Every child born of donor sperm or eggs is wanted and planned.

As part of her research into families where children are born by sperm donor, Dr Zadeh has seen a whole spectrum of attitudes and feelings towards donors. Some mothers want as much information as possible, whereas others have no curiosity about the donor. She's noticed that this is influenced by UK geography: if the family is based in an area where using a sperm donor is very rare, the mothers are likely to want to know the least. They might feel much more alone and that their choice is a lot more controversial in their circumstances. Some women she's met haven't told anyone at all how they became parents, except the researchers themselves. In these cases, they find it's easier to tell a different narrative publicly about a father's absence. To feel this level of stigma over your child's background must be really tough, and potentially complicated for the children too. But she's found that solo mums with donor-conceived children are more likely to have told their child about their origins by the age of eight than couples who have used a donor to help them conceive.

I understand why couples are often slower to tell their children: the father question isn't an obvious one, as it is with a solo mother.

Family backgrounds of solo-mum families are increasingly diverse. While in 2005 research showed that solo mums tended to be quite well off, today there are many mums who will borrow from the bank to have a child. There are fewer siblings than in more conventional families. And Dr Zadeh has found that the women she has met are remarkable.

'It looks really hard,' she says. 'These women aren't struggling, but if they want to get a pint of milk, the baby has to come, or if they want to have a shower, they need to work around their child – the day-to-day stuff is hard.' But she notes that many people with partners are in a similar situation. She has found that support networks are good for many solo mums; they might be fortunate enough to have a live-in nanny or live with their parents or a sibling.

She's researched whether coming from a one-parent family is destabilising for children. In the case of parents divorcing, children can suffer because of parental conflict, from their main carer being depressed and from a drop in financial circumstances. To my relief, Dr Zadeh tells me that it is divorce itself that causes the problems and that coming from a solo family is not the same: there is no difference between children in one-parent and two-parent families. Factors that can contribute to a slightly raised level of problems are increased financial stress and increased levels of parenting stress that mums feel, but this is irrespective of being in a one- or two-parent home.

Her latest study at the Centre for Family Research, which is run by world-renowned Professor Susan Golombok, involves approximately fifty single people and fifty couples, all who've used donors to conceive their children, who are aged up to twelve years old. In a small sample of nineteen of those children, she's found that the child's feelings towards the donor relates to the quality of their relationship with their mum. Those who feel most secure also feel most positive about their donor. Those who are less secure feel more negatively towards their donor.

She's also studied the media coverage of donor conception from the 1980s to today. Depressingly, coverage over the last four decades has barely evolved, and there are similar attitudes to the last century seen in some pieces today. In the 1980s and 1990s, there was a rhetoric around so-called 'virgin births', referring to women having babies through insemination or IVF, with many news articles about women being incapable of romantic relationships, asking how they will have an effective mother–child relationship if they aren't with a partner. Dr Zadeh's research suggests that the vast majority of women have had relationships prior to having their babies. In 2015, a popular newspaper ran a story under the same virgin birth headline. It reported that twenty-five straight women, who'd never had sex, had given birth in the last five years. Bishops, imams and psychotherapists shared their concerns at single women becoming parents without a partner, and whether these women who are fearful of close physical relationships will be unable to give their children love. One particularly enraging line reads, 'Campaigners for traditional families even said "the 'distorted' move turned babies into little more than 'teddy bears' to be 'picked off the shelf'"'. Articles like this show me that what I'm doing is still frowned upon by sections of society.

But Dr Zadeh doesn't know how much press coverage really affects solo mums. She has found that most of the people she's interviewed choose not to read the newspapers that they expect to have unsupportive, or reactionary, views.

I'm reassured by her research that there's no reason to believe that any solo-mum family will be any different from any other family, and that every family, no matter how it's constituted, has highs and lows, trials and tribulations, and there are a lot of ways that people have children today.

But I suspect that cultural perceptions of people choosing to use a sperm donor do have an effect on solo mums – especially while they are making the decision to become parents.

* * *

Even with the reassurances of Dr Zadeh, it would be misleading to say that I find early pregnancy a delight. I'm not
sick, but the worry is tough. I don't want to do anything that
might dislodge the fragile ovum – which is not how biology works but is certainly how my brain is working. I look
pregnant very quickly. People say that you look pregnant
more swiftly during second and third pregnancies. I don't
know whether my body remembered the rounded stomach
I'd had before my miscarriage two years earlier, or whether
I am simply eating so much to combat the exhaustion of the
hormonal shifts in the first three months of being pregnant.
I also really want to look pregnant – I want outward signs
of what is going on inside me to make it feel true: a swollen
belly is proof that a baby is growing within me. I want to do
everything in my power to make this real.

I have a couple of scans in the first couple of months to
check the little foetus is growing, but I remain anxious. I
want my baby to be safe inside so much that I find it hard to
relax. It's as if I believe that the only way my baby will come
into existence is if I will it with every cell in my body. I sense
that my family are also nervous on my behalf – I think they
are concerned that if anything goes wrong I'll be shattered.

My sister-in-law Jesscomes with me to my twelve-week
scan at the hospital. I have a blood test, sign lots of forms
saying that I am happy for all results to be used in research,
and go through to the scanning room. A gel is placed on my
bare tummy, and a Doppler run over it to pick up the ultrasound images of what is going on inside. The scan itself takes
almost an hour; the doctor is so thorough as he looks at each
body part, checking that my baby is developing as expected.
I cry when he spots the heartbeat, and keep my eyes closed
at first – scared, and reluctant to see life as a cluster of cells,
organs and arteries – but eventually I look at the screen for

myself. The little wriggler inside me doesn't seem to enjoy the scan, and keeps moving away from the Doppler every time it is placed on my tummy, making hard work for the doctor. He continues to reassure me that everything seems to be healthy, and gives me a prediction (with my encouragement) that my baby is likely to be female. It's something about the angle of the dangle at that age, before genitals are formed.

Half an hour after the scan, the doctor calls me back in to give me my blood test results. I have an unusually low level of PAPP-A hormone, a protein that is produced by the placenta. The doctor explains that this could cause growth problems, as it could be tricky for my baby to get enough nutrients from the placenta later in pregnancy. It also affects the probability of Edwards' syndrome and Patau's syndrome, which are measured along with Down's syndrome and are also caused by a chromosomal irregularity. Unlike Down's, these are severely life-limiting conditions that mean a baby is very unlikely to live to be more than a year old. The probability comes out as a high, one-in-eighteen chance. The doctor remains reassuring: he says that these conditions would have shown up on the scan as my baby's heart and brain would not be developing normally. But his reassurances can't quash the worry and stress that I feel. I am offered a blood test, which I accept, and time slows as I wait for the results.

I text Lucinda: 'I just hope it's okay. It's totally beyond my control, which I find hard, but hopefully will all work out.'

She replies to say, 'That's the hardest bit about pregnancy, and actually about babies, full stop, so maybe it's getting you in training.' A fortnight later I receive the blood test results. The chances that my baby has Edwards' syndrome or Patau's syndrome is a slim one in 10,000. But there is a very low level of the baby's DNA in my blood, which is consistent with the low levels of PAPP-A hormone and suggests the placenta isn't working very hard.

I also find out from the blood test that I am definitely making a daughter; the doctor's prediction was spot on. And I am delighted. Partly because, being a woman, I will hopefully understand her journey, but also because I love my two nephews so much already. Somehow it feels less likely that there will be any comparisons.

I am told to take an aspirin a day so that there will be an easy flow of blood from the placenta to my growing baby, and I have scans scheduled throughout the pregnancy to make sure my daughter is growing. I need to prepare myself for a tricky third trimester, and to get my head around the fact that I might be meeting my daughter earlier than ideal.

I'd hoped that after my twelve-week-scan I could relax. Instead, I feel stressed about my daughter's well-being and spend much of my time willing her to be happy and healthy inside me. While in life I would not wish averageness on anyone, in utero that is exactly what I wish for my daughter: that she will grow in a very average way.

6

Publicly Pregnant

The focus of my world has changed hugely: I'm ever aware of the baby growing inside me, but all around me life continues as it always has, which leaves me feeling slightly disconnected. I felt a similar sense of dislocation when my dad died, when it seemed quite incredible that people were continuing their day-to-day lives while I felt that I'd been flung around and the world had changed shape. Only, this time, life is changing in a cautiously optimistic way.

I've lived with housemates since moving back to London from Paris. Sharing my home seemed natural to me. Perhaps my love of long-term relationships helps me to appreciate the companionship and find it easy.

My housemates feel like family. We've made big decisions together, like whether we need a landline and (to my absolute horror) how to get rid of mice, and we share each other's successes, tough times and meals. We share celebrations: we scribble birthday messages on the chalk board in the kitchen for each other to wake up to, and we bake – or buy – good cake, and each December we decorate an almost ceiling-height tree that Ed drags up the road from the local Hungarian restaurant (which has a busy sideline), while drinking mulled wine.

We've been on campervan trips together across France and into Spain, and I used to share a commute with Ale, my Italian flatmate, who knows all the other Italians in the area and can spot people from her country in any crowd.

I've felt huge support from them since I explained my decision to try to have a child on my own. I don't think it's something that either of them would consider doing them-selves, but they make sure that I feel that I can turn to them to talk about anything.

My housemate Ed, a teacher, told one of his friends what I was planning. 'Features writers, they do all sorts of crazy things for their articles,' the friend said.

When I was three months pregnant, Ed and I took the van to Wales with a surfboard and a fire pit. Ed messed around in the waves while I relaxed on the beach. I didn't dare head for the waves in case one smacked the board into my tummy, and when some young boys kicked a football full pelt into my stomach I doubled over, then cried a few tears, not from pain so much as anxiety that I might miscarry.

The exhaustion of pregnancy makes me an unsociable flatmate. I have almost enough energy to go to work, and am just about able to get through the day, then once home I simply curl up. Sometimes on the sofa; sometimes in bed. I frequently hear Ed and Ale laughing about something or other from the kitchen as I'm lying in bed, and try to will my body into moving to find out what they're talking about and how their days have been. But my body rarely listens, and I usually wake up what feels like an hour later, to the sound of Ed getting ready for work, reminding me that I too should start my day.

I work at the *i* paper, a small British national newspaper based in west London. I am surrounded by journalists, keen observers of changes to the world around them who are employed for their ability to sniff out stories. But with pregnancy, people don't want to jump to conclusions. This is why people find it hard to offer a seat on trains unless a woman is wearing a Baby on Board badge – it's not ignorance, it's a fear of offending.

Although my editor at work knows I am pregnant, most other people in the office don't, officially. I dress in increasingly baggy clothes. I find it hard to think of anything besides pregnancy, and worry about the growing girl inside so much that friends and my mum suggest gently that the best thing for the baby is to be calm. Work, which has always played an important role in my life, fades into the wings: I am there, but it rarely fully occupies my mind.

One Sunday, I am in the office, helping to prepare Monday's paper. Newspapers on Mondays are usually slimmer than the rest of the week, with less advertising and pages to fill. Some stories will be written the week before, and the paper is put together by far fewer people than on other days. If all is quiet in the world – and no major news stories are breaking – it's more laid-back than during the week, so when I make a throwaway comment about being pregnant, almost everyone in the office comes to congratulate me. I feel scared receiving congratulations before my daughter is born – I don't want to tempt fate – but it also feels lovely to have my news, and my tummy, out in the open. At last, I can start wearing maternity clothes.

A couple of weeks later, I mention something about being single to one of my colleagues. 'I had no idea,' he tells me.

'I presumed you had a partner.' It's the logical assumption; when I see people with a pregnancy bump I too imagine a partner in the background, even though I'm going solo.

*   *   *

The heavy tiredness that I've felt over the past few months shows no sign of diminishing. I still feel completely wiped out. Friends who are mothers had promised I'd experience a bounce in energy when the placenta kicked in during the second trimester and my tiny daughter wasn't taking her nutrition directly from me. This didn't happen, so I start to accept that getting out of bed is incredibly hard and takes a great deal of effort. When I'm not in work, I frequently stay in bed to rest. Finally, a doctor tests my blood and finds that my lack of energy is because I've become very anaemic. I've just put it down to pregnancy.

Hormones make me upset and tearful at unpredictable times. I often feel a sadness that I can't enjoy my pregnancy or get excited about meeting my daughter because it's considered high risk. I get splitting headaches, and I'm concerned about my blood readings being all over the place. The laid-back glow I'd always imagined I'd have when pregnant is entirely absent. If I get pins and needles, I'm worried it is pregnancy related, rather than a result of leaning on my arm. If I have indigestion, I think I'm suffering from a terrible disease rather than simply being pregnant. And if I have tummy ache, I automatically worry about my little wriggler inside. Worst is when people tell me that worrying is bad for me and the baby – another thing to feel anxious about. Pregnancy isn't much fun – and nor am I.

But the scans themselves show my baby is developing as expected – the most important thing. And for twenty-four hours after each scan I feel calm – maybe even aglow – as

I know all is right with the world inside me. 'If only there were a little window looking into your tummy,' my friend Sarah says. 'Then you could be reassured the whole time.'

Pregnancy is such an introverted time as a mother's relationship with their unseen child develops. I hug a pregnancy pillow at night and watch my body change shape.

I feel hugely grateful to be pregnant but taken aback that I'm not loving every moment of it. Like so many people who know how it feels when pregnancy goes wrong, I don't dare relax into it too much in case it's taken away. Also, pregnancy for me is a waiting state: the joy to be found in it is mainly a projection of the future, and this is something I simply don't dare do.

So far, the only plus I can find to pregnancy – which feels like stepping into a nine-month chrysalis of hope – is that I get a seat on the crowded Tube. And since that is only gained after being shoved, pushed and prodded to get into the carriage itself, holding my arms like a shield, it feels like a justified consolation.

At times, I wish for a partner to reassure me (however untrue) that I am looking beautiful, rather than fat. I feel nostalgia for good relationships that I've had with boyfriends who were my sense of home, craving support as I travel into an unknown world.

But for every time I feel a yearning for someone to cuddle me or help me, or look after me so that I can concentrate on sitting on my sofa watching Netflix, I'm told by someone that they admire what I'm doing. I feel buoyed up by the encouragement of people around me, and so appreciate their comments.

One friend tells me expressly that she wishes she'd had her baby alone with a donor. 'It would have been so much easier,' she says. 'You don't realise how differently you want to bring up children until you're doing it. And you have to compromise.'

Another friend, whose marriage is choppy, says similar, but with more sadness. I've always thought that seeing the features of someone I love in the face of my child is an incredibly romantic thing, and perhaps they both did too, but it's the practicalities of life that are tough. She told me that their wonderful holidays would feel enchanted, but – as for many couples – they needed to be enough to offset arguments over lifestyles and values and the really mundane parts of life – washing machines and cleaning up – that can reduce a relationship to simply tolerating each other.

The man I married briefly insisted we got a cleaner when we first moved in together because life is too short to argue over whose turn it is to clean the toilet – it was a far better decision than the one we made to marry.

* * *

Christmas approaches, unusually sober. My emotions continue to run high. Each time I turn on the television and see charity-appeal adverts showing pictures of babies suffering I start sobbing, and send a text donation. I feel watery, leaky, and I want to protect not only my baby but every child.

This sense of guarding my future daughter informs my days. Some people are overprotective parents; I am an overprotective pregnant person. Glasses of wine remain undrunk, prawns uneaten, sushi shunned. I am very 1950s about pregnancy, as I'm so concerned about having another miscarriage.

I work in a building where lots of newspapers are bundled together on different floors. The *i* newspaper is on the first floor, the *Independent* and *Evening Standard* on the second and the *Daily Mail* and *Mail on Sunday* are on higher floors. People say that you can tell which newspaper someone works for by the way they dress, and there is an element of truth to that: people don't turn up to a job on the higher floors looking scruffy.

One late morning I look out of the glass doors of the *i* newspaper to see the reception area crowded with smartly suited workers. Gossip starts spreading: a rumour suggests that a letter has been sent to someone at the *Daily Mail*, claiming to contain anthrax. The floor where *Mail* staff work has been evacuated. The air conditioning is switched off so that it won't spread throughout the building. But we're all sitting at our desks, continuing to work. Colleagues are joking about how they will be getting the paper out whatever. Except me. My attitude to risk is totally at odds with my colleagues. I go outside to ask the policemen what is happening and they confirm that while they don't know what the white substance is, there is a concern that it could be anthrax. Perhaps it's pregnancy, perhaps it's simply common sense, but I wander off to a coffee shop until the commotion's died down. (I've not always been so risk adverse: on 7 July when I heard about the London bombings, I headed to Tavistock Square, the site of the bus bomb, to contribute to articles on the attacks.) And, of course, it isn't really anthrax. But I'm not up for taking any chances.

It's probably just as well that I start going to a pregnancy yoga class around this point; I hope to calm the anxious chatter in my mind. I love practising yoga, and during tough times in my life, such as when my dad died, I've found that it's helped to slightly slow the whirring of my thoughts. I've even taken part in yoga teacher training, and have always been drawn to an active practice: lots of flowing through vinyasas, with planks and downward-facing dogs, lots of twists and arm balances. The classes would end with a headstand or shoulder stand before savasana, the final resting pose in any yoga class where people lie on their backs and relax. None of these – apart from the final resting pose – feature in pregnancy yoga.

The first section of the class is more sociable than a standard yoga class. Each week we introduce ourselves, say how many weeks pregnant we are and talk about how our pregnancy is going. It's here that I learn about magnesium spray to help cramps, and how osteopaths can help with pelvic pain.

Then follows the active part of the class, where we stretch. I'm using 'active' in the most generous possible sense: to call this class gentle makes it sound more demanding than it is. But each week I find it getting slightly harder as my body continues to swell. And those people who are approaching the end of their pregnancies are getting as much of a stretch as anyone could want while carrying the equivalent of a water melon in their belly.

At both the beginning and the end of the class we take the time to breathe calmly and send love to our unborn babies. In my everyday life I find it odd and slightly stilted when I talk to my baby inside me, despite encouragement from midwives, though I love the thought of my baby getting to know my voice and the sounds of people important to me, so I really appreciate taking this time to feel a sense of connection with my unborn baby. My hippy sensibilities are overjoyed as I pictured the golden thread between her and me, and send her love and encouragement.

I chat lots to the other soon-to-be mums, and find that two other women are single and pregnant by sperm donors. Statistically, that is highly unlikely, but it's a self-selecting crowd of people who turn up to pre-natal yoga. I suddenly feel a lot less alone – and realise the importance of support from people in similar situations. I'm incredibly lucky to have friends and family who are carrying me through my pregnancy, but it is a relief to meet people who are also planning a solo-mum future. We're able to talk about the practicalities that lie ahead of us: decisions over who to have at our births; how we'll cope on our own; who will offer us support with a newborn.

One of the mums, Saskia, radiates calm and poise. I tend to admire people who are considered, because I can sometimes become fiery with determination and not think of consequences. I suspect she's either slightly self-conscious, or proud, of her age because she mentions that she may be a little bit older than me (though in reality she is only very slightly). She's very cool and speaks to me about how she came to be pregnant and single. I'm amazed how many echoes there are of my own experience. But she's been through a hugely arduous process to become pregnant, and it makes me realise that I only skimmed the surface of fertility treatments.

Saskia knew she wanted children, and when she was thirty-eight she found out that her fertility levels were very low. To have children, she'd have to freeze embryos. Increasing numbers of young women freeze eggs, but she was advised that there was no point in doing this – they wouldn't survive the freezing and thawing process – and her best chance was for them to be fertilised before they were frozen. She was shocked. So stunned, in fact, that she did nothing for a year.

She kept vacillating between going ahead with IVF, or letting it rest and putting the subject of children out of her mind. Eventually she decided that she'd find it too heartbreaking not to even try to have a child, so she stumped up the cash for one round of IVF treatment. At the time, she didn't know whether she was going to freeze embryos to use at a later time, or have them transferred straight back into her, known as a fresh cycle. She really just wanted to see what would happen to her body.

At the first clinic where she went for a consultation, the female consultant couldn't help herself yawning as she told Saskia how slim her chances were to have any success with IVF. She apologised, but Saskia says she felt so sensitive that the experience left her feeling really upset.

At a second clinic, she felt more reassured by her consultation with a doctor and started treatment. The hormones made her feel emotional and while her body didn't react badly, she remembers it as an intense time. When the clinic went to harvest her eggs, they found only one, and it didn't make a viable embryo.

She took a step back. She was thirty-nine and decided to get really fit before she turned forty. She started a new job, focused on her fitness, and was enjoying dating. She thought she was doing okay.

Then a good friend of hers had a baby, other friends were still falling pregnant and she realised that the familiar pain that she'd felt each time someone else had become pregnant over the last few years hadn't diminished at all. If she felt so emotional about her friends getting pregnant, and loved seeing their babies so much, she realised that perhaps she wasn't really that okay, as she couldn't have fully left behind the idea of having a baby of her own.

Her fortieth birthday gift to herself was a package of three rounds of egg stimulation and their transfer back into her uterus.

As she was embarking on the process, one of her good friends put her in touch with a friend of a friend who was also hoping to become a solo mum. They'd spend nights together looking through donor websites, trying to find a sperm donor. 'I was trying to switch off my Internet romance head: I wasn't looking for a partner for me, but a biological father for a child,' she says. I wasn't so concerned about any confusion while looking for a donor, reassuring myself – perhaps naively – that biologically we're drawn to people to procreate, so hopefully the people we think would make good partners would also be good parents.

On one of those nights, the donor hunters discovered a new sperm bank in the UK, and Saskia picked her donor.

From then, it took four years of stopping and starting to become pregnant: she is now forty-four. She found the rollercoaster of taking drugs to stimulate her ovaries; then going in for egg collection and waiting to see what quality the eggs were; then waiting to see if they fertilise; then finding out if the embryos were good enough quality to freeze, an exhausting process.

The whole experience left her feeling shaken. She was still thinking that she didn't want to be a single mother – she wanted to be a mother with a partner. So, while she felt that she wanted to go through the motions or she'd regret it, she was also hoping that in the meantime she'd meet a partner and they could adopt together, or he would have children anyway. When she realised the reality that this process had created embryos that had the potential to become her child, it shocked her.

In between periods of waiting to see if embryos were growing successfully, she tried dating, but found she was having unsatisfactory flings rather than meaningful relationships that could lead, a few years down the line, to having a family. Whether she was with a partner or not, she didn't want to miss her chance to become a parent, or to passively choose to not have a baby by simply letting the opportunity pass her by. Sometimes she'd date divorced dads, and would feel envious when they spoke about their children.

Another of her friends decided to become a single mum and asked for advice on sperm banks and clinics. Saskia was happy to share what she'd learnt through those nights of research. When, a month later, her friend described the donor she'd picked and his interests, Saskia realised that he sounded incredibly similar to the donor she'd chosen. A few questions more and she was able to confirm that if both of them managed to get pregnant, their children would be related.

But it was her friend who got pregnant very swiftly. Saskia felt happy for her but dejected: she'd had one failed embryo transfer at this point and wondered why it couldn't be her that was pregnant.

Her second embryo transfer took, and she became pregnant. But at the twelve-week scan the doctor discovered that the foetus had died. It was a missed miscarriage and left her feeling broken.

She had one vial of donor sperm left, and thought she had to use it if there was any opportunity. The doctors were able to harvest one more egg, but they warned Saskia two days later that it wasn't the best quality. And finally, despite all the consultants warning her that the odds were very slim, she became pregnant. When the doctors first measured her hormone levels in pregnancy they warned her it might well be a chemical pregnancy. Now, months later, she believes a miracle has taken place.

When she was eight weeks pregnant, she went on a holiday to Portugal. On the fourth day, she met a man to whom she felt an instant attraction. She was honest about not wanting to mislead him, and told him she was pregnant. Twenty-four hours later, when he'd digested the news, he told her he was comfortable having a relationship with her. After serious consideration, Saskia realised that she didn't have the emotional capacity to invest in a new relationship as well as the child she was expecting, so she decided to embark on motherhood solo.

Saskia helps me to understand the realities of declining fertility: there are women who fall pregnant naturally at forty-five, but they are very much an exception, it's far more common to experience swiftly diminishing eggs. And with my hormone levels indicating egg reserve measuring so low, I suspect that if I'd waited even a couple more years there would be no guarantee that I would have been as lucky as Saskia was. I feel a sense of relief that I didn't pause and try one more relationship before having fertility treatment.

I feel very grateful to meet someone at pregnancy yoga who is going through a similar experience to me – and find myself telling my yoga teacher that solo mums are like buses (and look like them too, in a pregnancy yoga class): none for ages and then three come along at once.

7

An Army of Support

I feel the first kicks while at work, soon after my twenty-week scan. When I'm tired I get an involuntary fluttering of my eyelid and blink to my eye. It feels like this is happening inside me. My first instinct is to scratch this twitch in my tummy, but I stop myself in case I hurt the little human growing inside me. I don't tell my colleagues what is going on, but instead I remain absolutely calm as our print deadline approaches and everyone around me becomes more focused. Everything starts to feel a lot more real. And I'm very aware that I'm not prepared at all. Not prepared for the responsibility that is hopefully coming my way, but also, definitely, not prepared for childbirth.

When I'm six months pregnant, my housemates move to a new home in the same neighbourhood. It feels like the end of an era: since moving back from Paris I've lived with friends and now − for a short time − I'll be living alone until my daughter arrives. It gives me time to sort my home ready for her arrival, and I'm now sleeping so much that

I would barely see my housemates even if we did all live under one roof. But it makes me realise how imminent her arrival is.

I have a pile of pregnancy books sitting on my bedside table, but I don't dare read them. Partly, I don't want to tempt fate. But also, these books feel a little like the health and illness section of any *Lonely Planet* or *Rough Guide* travel book: I will leaf through the malaria, dysentery, dengue fever symptoms and am likely to then worry whether I'm experiencing them. Sometimes, ignorance can be bliss, so, while I usually read through life, and I would expect myself to have read every last word of wisdom, I'm curiously resistant. The pages to these manuals remain unturned as each night I choose sleep over research. Instead, I sign up to a National Childbirth Trust (NCT) course and my hospital's pre-natal course.

The NCT runs courses for expectant parents, and frequently gets a bashing for ignoring all forms of childbirth except for natural labour with no pain relief (the *Today* programme has previously debated whether the NCT tells women the truth about childbirth). This wasn't my experience at all.

I sign up to a course in my local library, and send a note ahead to the course leader, Annie, explaining that I'm a solo mum so will be turning up on my own and that I hope this is okay. She replies with a welcome, and says that while the other people are turning up in pairs she has no idea whether they are couples or people offering future mums support at birth and beyond.

They are all couples. I rush to the library from work, and as I tentatively take a seat, one of the soon-to-be-fathers tells me his girlfriend is sitting there. I shuffle up. I could only feel more out of place if I wasn't pregnant.

It's easy to forget that there's anything at all unusual about my pregnancy as I'm going about my work and catching up with friends and generally being me. People probably assume, as I do with other pregnant women, that there's a partner somewhere, but that doesn't stop me being an independent person. Except at NCT. Here everyone is very much a pair, which is not surprising. Being confronted by a load of strangers who may or may not share little other than a similar due date makes for a daunting setting, and it must be easier to face with the sanctuary of a best friend or loved one. But I am going in cold, and I don't have someone with whom to share supportive glances, or raised eyebrows.

On our first evening, shivering in an annexe of our local community library, a group of four couples – and me – sit and introduce ourselves to each other. I explain that I'm a solo mum. One of my least favourite things about London is that people sometimes ask how you spend your working hours before they've even found out your name. At NCT, it's different. Even after a month of getting to know each other, I could tell you where the couples are giving birth, whether they're expecting a girl, boy or surprise, and their due dates, but I have only the vaguest of idea of how they spend their days.

Annie, our course leader, is an artist who studied at Goldsmiths University and is a mother of three. She is wonderfully supportive and enthusiastic, though I suspect her creativity is somewhat wasted on decorating nappies with mustard, Marmite and piccalilli to teach us all about the differing shades of baby poo.

She tells us that we might not imagine it now, but that we're all going to become great friends, and are likely to be in touch with each other all the time. We all look around at each other. I don't think I'm imagining that the slight suspicion I'm feeling is reflected on the faces of my classmates.

She says she understands how uncomfortable it might be to

sit on chairs at this stage of pregnancy, so she says that we're welcome to bring cushions, lie on the floor, or anything else that might help. She also points to the bathrooms, knowing that heavily pregnant women spend a significant proportion of their day in toilet cubicles.

The first week of the course shows me how little I know about having a baby. I've been in denial. I've been so focused on getting pregnant and how I'm going to look after my daughter that I've totally forgotten that she's got to make an entry into the world. There's no way round it, and – however it's dressed up, even with baby dolls – it's terrifying.

We are divided into three groups. Annie splits us into groups of three and mixes up partners; I'm part-grateful, part-relieved that she is making sure I feel included, and not like the single gatecrasher. We are asked to explain the three stages of childbirth. Luckily, one woman in our group, who I later find out works as a radiologist in hospitals, knows the answers.

I'm clueless about what labour entails. I know many friends who've experienced it, all have survived and some feel more battle-wounded than others, but the details of what my body does are a mystery to me. If I'm honest, until we were asked, I didn't even know there were three stages to labour. It turns out that childbirth is another worry I can confidently add to my list, and it's somewhere near the top.

The first worry is whether I'll survive childbirth. I know millions have, but it appears there are no guarantees. Secondly, who will be with me? I don't want to approach what could, after all, be my dying moments alone. This isn't a fear that anyone else in my NCT class shares; instead they want their partners to keep their phones close by at work. But one thing I suspect we're all worried about, but don't dare to voice, is whether our babies will arrive healthy.

Each week, we meet at the library, getting to know each other a little through the prism of our massive stomachs.

When Annie teaches us massage that could be good in labour, she pairs up with me. This is amazing, as I get to observe everyone else trying to work out what's a good level of pressure, what's annoyingly light, and what's just plain annoying, while I receive a great massage to my lower spine. But I'm the least likely of everyone to be offered a soothing massage during labour.

We practise changing nappies and dressing dolls in vests and sleep suits, and we go through all the different types of drugs on offer to mothers during birth. We all say that we are hoping to have natural births, and Annie steps in with some sound advice: these drugs are here to help when people need them. This isn't a party – people rarely set out thinking they'll take all the drugs – but they can provide much-needed relief. It's heartening to hear that she doesn't feel a drug-free labour is some kind of badge of honour.

One week we're all asked about our hopes for the birth. I listen to a couple who talk about the benefits of hypno-birthing, which reframes labour so that contractions become surges that you ride as waves. They seem relaxed and are looking forward to childbirth – the complete oppo-site to me. They're young enough to be the first in their friendship group to have children, so they aren't scarred by tales from friends, but I wonder if the positive hypno-birthing breathing they're practising is helping too. The other couples seem to be aiming simply for healthy babies, healthy mothers and parents who aren't too traumatised by the experience.

I share my dilemma about who will be with me for the birth of my daughter. Everyone listens in silence: this isn't a choice that they need to make.

I explain that I've turned down my mum's offer to be there. I think we would both spend our time trying to protect each other. I wouldn't want to appear scared in case I worried her, and wouldn't be able to relax because I'd want to shield her. Which is ironic, since she knows what labour entails. But I have no doubt that she'd also be trying to hide her emotions from me, and between the two of us we'd be too polite for labour to happen. Also, if I end up screaming and swearing I'd ideally like it not to be aimed at my mum: I'll be relying on her kindness after my daughter's born, so I don't want to use up any goodwill before I've even left hospital.

A couple of friends have also offered to be there for the birth, which I hugely appreciate, but one lives in Belgium and the other lives an hour away, works full time, has two children and a husband who works late into the evening. I don't know whether my daughter is going to be a good timekeeper; my friend could be on standby for weeks, and arranging that much backup childcare sounds stressful. Neither seems the most practical solution.

I say that I'm hoping to find a good doula. Until I was pregnant I'd never heard of a doula: a woman who offers their support in childbirth. They're not trained midwives, but are trained to help women giving birth.

Some people choose the support of a doula in addition to their partner – I imagine this is especially useful if your partner gets queasy or is prone to panic, or if you simply think an extra, calming presence will be helpful.

For me, I feel she'll be playing a crucial role as the person responsible for helping me through what could be a choppy few hours or days, so I want to pick well.

At this point my NCT teacher steps in and recommends a doula in south-east London.

I meet up with her after work one Friday night. I'm already reeling from just starting to consider birth, so perhaps I don't have clear lenses when I meet her.

She sits me down on her sofa, with her cat and her son, who I guess is around ten years old. And then she proceeds to chat to me about all aspects of having a baby. I feel inhibited by the presence of her son, and alarmed by her ethos on birth.

'Women have been giving birth with no intervention for thousands of years,' she tells me. Which is true, but in ancient times many died in the process. And even though it's so incredibly rare now, the health of both me and the little human inside me is my biggest fear about childbirth. She sounds so suspicious of doctors that I have an image of being told by medics that I need a life-saving medical intervention and her blocking the way to protect my right to give birth naturally.

She talks about forceps delivery, which saved my life as I was coming into this world, and says that babies end up with terrible headaches that can make breastfeeding very hard, which will then have a knock-on effect on the child's well-being. She's possibly right, but since no one chooses a forceps delivery, it seems a little harsh to suggest that a not-to-plan birth will have such a terrible effect on someone's life.

I start feeling incredibly stressed, and eventually tell her that nothing has made me feel more tempted to have a planned Caesarean section. I think it's fair to say that neither of us are convinced by each other. I'm really upset, and talk to my pregnancy yoga teacher Michele about my experience in our next yoga class. I find out that Michele is training to be a doula. She hasn't yet assisted a birth, but I already know her and feel comfortable with her, and I ask whether she might consider being there for the birth of my daughter. She's a lot more down to earth about the whole birth process, and while she supports my wishes for a natural water birth with midwives for support rather than doctors, she's absolutely not going to bar medical intervention if it's going to be helpful for me or my baby.

My sister-in-law, Jess, also volunteers to be there, and I'm relieved to take her up on the offer. It's all very well to expect a partner to step up to a labour – they helped get you into it after all – but I don't think it's fair to give my sister-in-law that sole responsibility. It's definitely not something she signed up for when she met my brother. By having Michele there, if Jess can't be around for any reason, or wants a break while I'm trying to push, then she'll know that I'm being looked after.

Jess has had two children herself, and after an emergency scramble the first time she is a cheerleader for C-sections. But she's prepared to humour me as I write out my birth plan including a water birth, with hypnobirthing and lavender oil to keep me calm.

'This sounds more like a spa trip than a birth,' she says.

One thing Michele suggests is that Jess and I come along to her birthing workshop, so we do. And while all the couples are learning about good positions to give birth in, and that lying on your back is the way people give birth only on telly programmes, not in reality, we both start giggling.

It starts when all the birth partners are told to sit behind those of us who are pregnant and put their arms around our bumps. Everyone else is, presumably, in love, and affectionately leans in to their partner and future child. As they are feeling in tune with each other and their babies, Jess and I join in very awkwardly.

Jess hasn't had a good feel of my bump at all over the last seven months. She's amazingly supportive and drops round for cups of tea regularly, which I appreciate, but there's no bump stroking. And she already loves to tease me for my hippy ways, so I know this is giving her ammunition for at least the next decade.

Our giggles get worse – I can't do anything except laugh. Maybe it's nerves about birth, maybe it's awkwardness, but I become incapable of giving off a cool, independent single-mum-to-be vibe. I'm desperately trying to stifle my giggles, worried that the couples will conclude that I'm too silly and immature to have a baby, but this makes it worse.

Planning for such a pivotal moment, the moment from when I'll never be free of responsibility again, is overwhelming. And the only way to get there is by putting myself in the most vulnerable position a human can be in. I can understand why labours are said to stop during earthquakes and natural disasters: it's going to be quite hard enough without walls crashing down around me.

Michele can see my discomfort and says it's good to laugh, and slowly I manage to calm down from mild hysteria.

We go through different positions that can help for birth, from being on all fours to rocking against a wall. Jess uses a massage ball to roll up and down my back, and presses down on my sacrum, both of which can sometimes feel good in early labour; I experiment with squatting while pulling down on a scarf draped over a door, and sitting on a birthing ball. Michele gives everyone massage oil, but also warns all the partners that a woman in labour may not want to be touched at all, and not to take it personally if so. I think Jess is more likely to feel relieved than offended.

By the end of the session, we definitely feel a lot more comfortable with each other. Jess can even touch my tummy without me collapsing in laughter. But I decide I'll pack a bikini top for the birthing pool – if she's going to have to see my vagina, I'll at least cover up my breasts – so I'm not *that* uninhibited.

8

Stigma

I jump in an Uber to take me to my final, thirty-six-week scan.

'Girl or boy?' the driver asks.

'Girl,' I reply.

'You're lucky – and what does your husband think of that?'

'I haven't got a husband,' I tell him, noting that he's several decades older than me.

'Ah, your boyfriend then?' he replies.

'Errrr, I think he's pleased,' I say.

Am I making an assumption that he might be more traditional than me, and am I trying to protect him? Or am I just trying to protect myself from his judgement? I think my reluctance is more than just laziness: perhaps a ten-minute drive isn't enough time to explain how and why I'm having a baby on my own.

But after all this time carrying my baby, and being so open about what I'm doing, why am I worried about explaining myself? Perhaps I don't want him – or anyone – to feel pity for me or my daughter when this was a conscious decision. Or perhaps there is still a little bit of me that would find it reassuring to have a partner in the background – someone who wants to share this journey with us. I'm aware it's the first time that I've directly lied to a stranger; I've let some people make assumptions, but I've never misled before.

At my scan I have a weigh-in, and for the first time someone comments on how much my petite frame has swollen up. I agree; I look like a Violet Beauregarde blueberry. My determination to look pregnant at three months now means I'm huge.

I lie down and lift up my shirt so that I can be scanned. I know the routine now: cold gel on my tummy; look away from the screen until I hear encouraging words and then get more and more fascinated with how my daughter's doing inside. I'm told that she is growing consistently, then I'm shown a three-dimensional picture – a scanner's party trick – where I see her perfect face with a nose squished up against my pelvis. I feel ready to meet her, to get to know her, and unbelievably lucky to be able to embark on this journey together with her.

I know we're both surrounded by love, though not of the most conventional sort from a partner and dad. But love can come from anywhere, and just because it doesn't come in a standard box doesn't make it any less uplifting or wonderful, or less likely to help see us through.

I feel hugely lucky to have received support rather than disapproval from those I love. I am aware that my mum is worried on my behalf: I think she's concerned that the baby might not survive, and that I don't have the strength to go through a tragedy of this sort alone. I too am reluctant to buy lots of baby clothes in case it's tempting fate. But her worries stem from love, not disapproval.

I'll never know whether people are less progressive in reality than they are to my face; whether friends out in pubs (while I've stayed home, feeling very sober indeed) have gossiped about their mate who's having a baby alone using a donor. But my friends are a liberal bunch, and I can't imagine that any of them would see it as scandalous. Somehow it doesn't seem important to me. The only negativity I experienced was when a friend who lives in Devon got in touch to tell me that a couple of mutual friends – whom I know only distantly – had been speaking about me on New Year's Eve in the pub. They'd been talking about how I got pregnant and making jokes about sperm in a bucket. It all sounded really unpleasant. I was upset, and also couldn't work out why someone would tell me that their friends were being so mean. Surely it would have been better to tell them why it's offensive instead? The conversation left me feeling unsettled, in the way I did as a teenager – and then I remembered that I'm not an adolescent and I've got a baby to grow. If I want to worry, I can simply picture childbirth. I don't need to cast my mind to a group of men with old-fashioned views.

In contrast, my ninety-year-old grandparents are supportive of my choice: my French grandmother is more disapproving of me eating steak well cooked in pregnancy (and ruining delicious meat) than of having a child conceived by sperm donor.

I've been carried by the support, love and admiration I've received. If I'd done this a few decades ago, I suspect it would have been a lot harder.

My mum's neighbour, Madeline, had children by sperm donor twenty-five years ago. She was in her mid-thirties, and although she'd had relationships with men, she realised she was a lesbian and very much wanted to be a mother.

Her first approach was to ask a gay friend to donate his sperm. He took an HIV test and they tried for several months, with him passing her sperm in jam jars. Madeline would monitor her cycle closely so that she knew when she was ovulating, at which point her friend had to perform, swiftly. It was fraught with problems: on one occasion her friend arrived just minutes before her brother unexpectedly called by, to show her his new car. It was difficult to feign interest in the vehicle while wondering how much longer the sperm would last, in a jar, under her armpit to keep warm. Doing the procedure herself was difficult and she had no success.

Madeline needed a new plan. She'd lost several friends through AIDS and so sleeping around was not on the cards. She asked a single heterosexual friend, who was already a father, to help her. She explained to him that she wasn't looking for commitment, but to get pregnant. But the experience was very stressful and the process really confirmed her own sexuality. She tried for several months before deciding it was too much.

At this point Madeline eventually decided to register at a clinic and had the necessary interviews. A very short while later in 1991, the tabloids ran headlines about 'virgin births', lambasting women for getting pregnant on their own. The clinic called to explain that they were no longer going to be helping single women but did suggest another agency, which was happy to sign her up after more interviews.

Very quickly, through this clinic, Madeline became pregnant with her daughter.

Not everyone approved of her decision, and she did encounter prejudice. When she went to hospital for a pregnancy check-up, a doctor gave her a big lecture about the immorality of what she was doing, which she found upsetting while feeling vulnerable already. She had a strong relationship with both her parents, but when she gave them the news, her mum thought she'd be in shame for the rest of her life. She suggested that her daughter could go on a holiday around the world; she was worried she'd be ostracised for the rest of her life.

Madeline had to explain that it had taken her a long time to get to this point. Once her mother had accepted it, she offered her support, taking her to John Lewis to get some nice things for the baby. And later, she commented that she couldn't believe how understanding people are. 'But when you've got a little baby, whatever its origin, it's a dear, treasured little individual,' Madeline says.

She believes she was lucky to be living in London, with its enormous diversity and different family groupings, and where she met many like-minded people through post-natal groups. She does remember, however, being at a swimming class and another mum asking about her baby's dad. Madeline explained that she'd deliberately become a single parent. The mother she was chatting to found it so unpalatable she literally just swam away.

Almost as soon as Madeline's daughter was born, she had an overwhelming wish to create a brother or sister for her so that she had someone else in her generation. She didn't get pregnant quickly this time, and it was a more medicalised, intrusive experience than with her daughter because she had injections to encourage hormones.

Three years later, she became pregnant with her son. They are half-brothers and sisters, because she wasn't asked whether she wanted to keep sperm from the same donor to potentially make a sibling; in the 1990s clinics matched eye colour, hair colour and skin colour, and if you were lucky, they told you the donor's profession (frequently 'student').

She thinks it's a great shame that sperm donors were

anonymous at the time and is very pleased that the law has finally changed. She hopes that in the future, society will catch up and be entirely accepting of people being who they are and of all the different types of family.

Madeline was always completely open and straightforward with her children, and says that she found it easier to chat to them about their origins – because they always knew – than coming out to them as gay, as she realised belatedly that her children had presumed she was straight, and she'd somehow presumed they'd always known her sexuality. 'It didn't cross my mind. They knew gay friends of mine, but it had never come up about myself – and it was years later that I explained it to them.'

She didn't have partners as her children were growing up, although her exes were very much still in her life, and one is an honorary godmother. But she isn't sure how she'd have shared the disciplining of the children anyway. 'It's quite tough if someone comes in and wants to input into it,' she says. 'With two little ones your hands are full, you don't feel you're missing out too much on relationships.' While she'd never describe her experience as a bed of roses, she says that she's so benefited from having children, and she feels that as long as there are lots of friends around, the children don't miss out on anything by being donor conceived.

She has never regretted her decision for a moment and thinks that because she got pregnant alone so very deliberately she'd done a lot of soul-searching, ensuring she knew what she was taking on. As an older mother she was more patient and had a lot more to offer her children.

I'm aware that Madeline's decision was a much bigger one than I've made, because two decades ago society was less supportive of single mothers, whether by chance or by design, and more homophobic, both openly and behind closed doors. But I hope that I can follow her lead and use age to my advantage, helping me to be patient.

While I've been lucky with the support I've received, it would be naive to take it for granted that people all have an easy ride today. There are those who choose to hide their children's history because they're worried that others won't accept it, and there are people whose families and friends upset and disappoint them by offering judgement rather than support. This is what Gillian – a friend of one of my close friends and a solo mum – found from one family member when she had her son almost two years ago. In her thirties, she was on the opposite end of the maternal spectrum to me: while I eye up other people's babies with longing, she thought they were dirty, sticky and annoying, and she couldn't see any attraction in having one. She had no presumption that she'd become a mother, but thought that if she fell in love she might feel differently about it.

Her instinct was right. At forty-six, she got married, and at forty-eight she got divorced. But, she says, the light of parental longing had switched on and she couldn't turn it off.

She found it incredibly hard to decide whether to have a child or not, but says she found the decision-making process fascinating, gruelling and ultimately impossible. She tried using logic, but found that columns in a spreadsheet don't work when it comes to creating a child because she found no active good reason in its own right. She questioned whether she really wanted a baby or whether it's because society is woven around children and it made her feel like a misfit, or because someone had told her she couldn't have a child, or an unexplainable biological urge. In the end, she just closed her eyes and went for it.

Time was running out: most European countries have a cut-off date for fertility treatment when women hit fifty.

Gillian got pregnant straight away. She used a donor egg and donor sperm and it was completely anonymous, in Spain. She only has key biological details about each donor, and feels this is the best way.

Although we don't know how widespread genetic testing is likely to be by the time her son is an adult (it's growing rapidly, and I can only imagine it will be standard practice in a decade as more treatments are tailored to individual bodies) she feels that, for now, she's cut off his choice and he has little hope of tracing his donors.

Gillian's only concern is that her son grows up knowing how very loved he is by his mother, rather than investing in genetic donors who are likely to be disinterested in him. She feels that tracing donors is 'trying to make a family out of something that never was, and pumps up expectations of children'. She says that she has no confusion over a sperm donor and a father, and a donor is 'a million miles away from a father'. I agree with her about this, dad could be a verb – it's about being active in a child's life.

She's surprised, though, at the level of respect she's observed some solo mums pay to their children's heritage, and was taken aback when she met up with one woman who was teaching herself Spanish because of the donor's origin. She makes me wonder how much a child's donor's history is important given the donor isn't in their life: is it cultural or do their origins count in their own right? I'm a mix of English, Welsh and French, and these all feel hugely important to me, but would they if I'd been brought up somewhere else, knowing this was my genetic history but with a parent who identified with another country? It's impossible to know, and while I feel that I place more weight on genetic history than Gillian, I can see why to her it seems so irrelevant when we're so shaped by the culture surrounding us as we grow up. It wasn't until I lived in France as an adult that I realised how British I am.

Part of being a mum is working it out as we go along, doing our best by our children, and when it comes to issues of identity, I think especially so for solo mums.

When Gillian decided to become a solo mum, she never considered that her stepfather would react badly to the news. During her pregnancy, he told her that she'd caused him illness and unhappiness. It came out of left field, and Gillian found it really hard to cope with it, as she was so shocked. Her mother, who died in 2009, would have been overjoyed, she says, and she suspects she would have threatened to divorce him for his reaction. While she was pregnant, he refused to acknowledge her son as his grandchild, which she found very difficult indeed.

Six months after her son was born, her stepfather had a heart attack. Gillian went to visit, and he was seemingly friendly to his grandson.

'He's the last dinosaur of his kind. I imagine that women will experience these attitudes less and less,' she says. They exchanged a series of letters, and finally he has recognised her son as his grandchild, but she feels the damage has been done, and their reconciliation brings little comfort.

In contrast, she experienced little stigma from doctors and midwives, and says her midwife tried to say that she'd met lots of new mothers of her age (she was fifty when she gave birth), which she thought was a little ridiculous when in 2012 there were 142 babies in total born to women aged fifty and over, so it seems statistically unlikely.

She's found parenthood a lot less onerous than she'd expected. When Gillian was growing up, her mother, a wonderful woman, was unable to protect her children from being aware that their father, with whom they all had an uneasy relationship, mistreated her emotionally and was disinterested in them. Having experienced this as a child, Gillian expected to find it very hard work bringing up her son; even though as a single mother she knew she wouldn't face such issues, she suspects it left a lasting vague fear. It has come as a pleasant discovery to experience the reality. She finds it a joy that her life has changed completely, and she is happy to look for different things out of holidays and socialising (though she hasn't yet been out dancing since before her son was born and hopes to very soon).

The downside of being a solo parent is that she'd love to share the joy of her son with someone. But she thinks it's unlikely that she'll meet anyone: with a man her own age the chances are they will have grown-up children and may not want to go through it again. She feels quite lonely – and she doesn't think there's an antidote to that. She makes me question why I feel so optimistic about meeting a partner in the future. I suspect having a child will filter out those who have never wanted children in their lives, but that doesn't bother me at all.

Gillian says that her son plugs the gap; she's always occupied, but it's different from an intimate relationship. She's proud to have survived a year back in her demanding job, plus renovating her house, alongside looking after her son. She's eminently capable, but her priorities are clear: when her son was hospitalised last January for nine days, she could only think of him. She doesn't think twice about completely dropping the work for which she used to finish at 11.30pm most nights before having a child.

Part of her consideration of becoming a solo mum at fifty is that she'll be seventy when her son is twenty. But, she says, apart from the fact that she'll die when he's relatively young, she feels completely fit and capable. And there are benefits to being an older mum: she's calmer and more confident than at twenty, and finances aren't such a concern. She says she doesn't know whether this makes up for her age. It's a worry I share. The decision to nurture a child is such a big one that only death can get in the way of it. And if it does, in an untimely way, there isn't a partner as a backup. But I think this is a major fear for anyone becoming a parent, whether they are single or not, because grieving parents struggle hugely too.

Her advice is to stop fretting about being good enough mum material: lots of women have children, they haven't killed their children and you don't have to be a superstar. I appreciate her no-nonsense attitude.

In contrast, I think the only time in pregnancy that I feel genuinely relaxed is immediately after a scan. I feel confident that my daughter is enjoying herself, growing averagely, and all is going well. After a day elapses, nagging worry starts to creep back in. Is she doing okay in there? Why can't I feel any kicking?

If a baby stops kicking for any length of time, it is dangerous, and this becomes something I feel I need to monitor constantly, especially as I approach the final weeks and days of pregnancy. I'm so close to meeting her.

It would be wonderful to have a non-neurotic partner at these times who could tell me not to worry — to be sympathetic, and to join me if it needs checking out. Instead, I let these worries flutter through my tummy.

If I become really alarmed, I visit the maternal assessment unit, which is a little drop-in centre in south London, attached to the hospital where I hope to give birth.

Each time I can't feel kicking I follow a pattern of drinking cold water, and waiting to see if that does the trick and startles my daughter into wakefulness. If that doesn't have an effect, then I drink Lucozade or eat chocolate (it's no surprise I've swelled so much). If neither the cold of the water nor the sweetness of sugar get my daughter dancing in my belly, I trudge over to the drop-in centre where the most friendly of midwives spend their time monitoring women, putting belts around their tummies to measure heartbeats.

My friend, Lizzy, is having a daughter three weeks after me, and we text each other sharing concerns.

'I'm having a paranoia day today. Can't really feel her move. Don't know if I should go to hospital,' she texts.

'Have you tried super-cold water?' I reply. 'She's prob asleep but the cold water will wake her up. My daughter must get fed up being woken up all the time.'

'She's awake. And moving. It'll be nice when they're actually here and we can see them, prod them to check they're okay.'

'I suspect I'll be that person who keeps waking my daughter up just to check she's okay – when she'd be okay if only someone didn't keep waking her up.'

Fortunately, I'm frequently distracted from how my baby's doing inside me by her imminent arrival outside. Friends and family are incredibly generous in donating buggies, slings, play mats, Moses baskets and clothes. One of my former bosses, Nik, empties out her entire attic and gives me a car load of baby bits to show her support for my choice to have a baby alone. I'm constantly taken aback by the support I feel – a whole army of women are propping me up.

I start winding down from work, spending more time on my sofa. The yoga classes that I found so gentle are now as challenging as I can manage. I feel a sense of urgency to get everything done – from boring bill paying, to fixing up my van to make it baby friendly, to visiting friends – as if I'll never have a chance to do anything again. Maybe this is my version of nesting, but it feels like I've got a looming deadline and have to get my world in order before it hits.

I buy raspberry leaf tea and pineapple, make curries and start walking down my stairs sideways. I'm scared of labour but I want to meet my daughter now. And time stills, going almost as slowly as it did in those first weeks when I was checking for a positive test result and willing myself to be pregnant.

I wait. And wait. And wait.

9

Meeting My Daughter

There's a narrative in our society that as soon as you have a baby you'll absolutely love them. It puts huge pressure on people: some friends who are brilliant mothers tell me it took time to warm to their children. One explains how ambivalent she felt towards her second child when he was born, and how conflicted she was when she saw her older daughter sitting on her bedroom floor, weeping at the arrival of her brother. How could she celebrate the arrival of a baby she needed to protect when it was the cause of this hopeless sorrow in her older child, whom she also needed to protect? She's a fantastic mother to them both, and I appreciate the warning that falling in love with my child might not be an immediate firework display, but can be more gradual.

I meet my daughter while lying on an operating table. My plans for a water birth had – like so many birth plans – gone awry. All the serious decisions I'd made ahead of the event about which aromatherapy oils to bring and which soundtracks to play during different stages of labour were completely redundant.

Astrid seems comfortable inside of me, and in no rush to get out. The doctors decide that it's time for her to join us in the world, and I'm induced – which means they put some sort of hormones into my vagina to try and encourage my body to go into labour. After a twelve-hour wait, my contractions start coming thick and fast. It's 11pm, and Jess is dozing. I want her to get some sleep before I need her help later on, but I am uncomfortable, so I walk to the desk to ask for some painkillers.

I hear someone making guttural sounds.

'She's not coping that well,' a friendly midwife tells me as I look at her in alarm. 'She's only two centimetres dilated.'

If that's the pain of two centimetres, I'm not sure how I'll get to ten centimetres. I'm suddenly not sure I'm up for labour after all. I go back to my bed and wait for the midwife to bring me some painkillers.

Half an hour later, she arrives with the medication.

'How's the woman in the next room?' I ask.

'Oh, she's had her baby. She dilated really quickly – she only just got to the labour ward in time,' the midwife explains. If only I'd known that earlier. But by this point, my contractions have slowed right down – I think they've been scared off. And they never pick up again. As morning comes, the consultant looks at my notes and says: 'Let's have you meet your baby today.'

I'm booked in for a C-section, taken upstairs to an operating theatre, and, after signing my consent, an anaesthetist injects my back to numb by body. While Jess dons scrubs to come into the operating theatre with me, my doula Michele remains outside, and tries to create the atmosphere I'd hoped for during childbirth. She gets out the scented oils, and is told by a nurse that they might be off-putting for other patients. I think she feels disappointed that it's so far from my intended hippy water birth as she packs away her spritzers.

Meanwhile, inside the operating theatre an impressive team work together, the radio playing in the background, to get my daughter to meet me safely.

I tell the anaesthetist that I'm not going to be able to feel emotional, as I can't feel my diaphragm when I breathe, which feels scary. Over and over again, I keep saying, 'I don't like this; I'm looking forward to it being over.'

I'm mid-flow when the curtain hiding my stomach is lowered just slightly; my baby is pulled out above so that I can see her enter this world.

She is rushed to the corner of the room for checks. They seem to be going on for a while. More people run into the operating theatre.

'Is everything okay?' I ask Jess.

'Yes, yes,' she replies.

Still my daughter isn't brought over to me. I feel that something is wrong. But I know she had come out pink – I'd already seen her momentarily. I continue clenching Jess's hand.

Then the midwife comes over with my daughter in her arms. She's laid upon me. So much for feeling no emotion: I cry with delight and joy.

The midwife explains that my baby hadn't started to breath immediately, so she'd called for all the paediatric doctors in the hospital to come and help. But when she wafted oxygen under her nose it had been enough for her to start breathing. No resuscitation was needed.

My daughter lies across my chest, my arms around her, for the remainder of the operation. I stop complaining then about not liking being cut open, and totally forget to be worried that I'm about to die, and just let the surgeons get on with their job while I cuddle my tiny, new baby.

And while I'd been warned that it might not happen, I immediately feel a huge burst of love for my daughter. I can't believe how lucky I feel to be given this girl, that I get to look after her and love her, and that she's my family. I name her Astrid Freya.

I'm wheeled into the post-operation recovery room, and soon I'm moved to the post-natal ward. My mum and Michele come to visit.

If you have a partner, it might feel intrusive having mid-wives coming to check up on you every few hours while you're spending time learning what it is to be a family. For me, I welcome their arrival and feel that they are cocooning me and my daughter in their love.

On my first night, just a few hours after my operation, they help me walk through the ward to have a shower. I take tiny steps in what feels like a completely strange body, half numb, so assaulted by surgery. The midwives sit me on a stool, washing my hair and body for me. I wouldn't have been able to do it alone, and it feels like the ultimate act of kindness.

Midwives help me learn how to breastfeed, spending hours showing me how to get my daughter to latch onto my nipples. They reassure me about any concerns, and help me get my lively baby to sleep when I'm struggling to stay awake. I sleep so lightly, with my eye on the transparent plastic hospital cot next to my bed. I don't want to miss a moment with my daughter.

At one point, I'm rocking Astrid while standing up and have slept so little that I keep feeling as if I'm going to fall. The midwives tuck Astrid up in bed with me, safely, and suggest we both get some sleep. It's something I'd have never done myself, unsure of what is safe for babies, and it is wonderful to be looked after.

I've never spent a night in hospital before and had previously thought of them as bleak places. I'd spent a lot of time going to cancer appointments with my dad when he was dying, so it surprises me that I opt to spend an extra night in the post-natal ward, but I feel that we're in the safest of hands. I'm very new to this, and these midwives seem to know what they're doing. I'm glad I do stay: Astrid cries and cries through the night and midwives come, explain that she's hungry and I don't have enough milk yet, and give her some formula. She immediately calms. They tell me that in a few days she'll just need and want breast milk, but that it will take a little time. It teaches me that there's no point in deciding how to parent until faced with the reality: I'd presumed that only breast milk would pass Astrid's lips, but I want what is best for my daughter.

When I'm finally discharged, my brother Henry and Jess come to collect me to drive me home to my flat. Henry helps me wrap Astrid up for her first experience of true daylight, of life outside. I leave the hospital with a bag of medication, and with my daughter. I somehow can't quite believe that I'm allowed to walk out with her.

I sit next to Astrid in the car, protective of her and feeling that constant observation is the best way to keep her alive.

At my flat, I feel a sense of shock. How am I going to look after my daughter on my own? She is the most precious, important thing in my world and I want to do the best by her. My brother and Jess leave, and I settle in for cuddles, feeling as if Astrid and I are absolutely alone in this world. An hour later, my mum arrives with a suitcase to help look after us for a couple of days so that I can learn how to be a mum.

My mum is one of the most loyal women that a daughter

or son could ever wish for. When I travelled across Asia after university she was worried that I'd run into trouble, and she definitely would have preferred it if I hadn't packed a backpack and left for a couple of years, apart from a few visits home. But she was also proud, because that's what I'd chosen, and when other parents told her what careers their children were pursuing she'd ask whether they might get a chance to travel. So, while she was worried that because I had chosen to become a solo mum I wasn't picking an easy life for myself, she also supported me completely. Her biggest fear was that I'd lose Astrid at birth, and I'd be broken, completely, by the experience.

My mum lives a few miles down the road, and has never slept over at my flat before. She had originally suggested that I come and stay with her, but I feel it's important to learn how to be a mother in my own home. But it all feels slightly awkward. I mainly want to sit and cuddle my daughter all day, and learn who she is and how to look after her. My mum knows very well how to look after a baby, but she finds that when she makes suggestions I'm prickly: I don't want her stepping into the role of a pseudo-partner.

Also, things change between generations. My mum wouldn't have dreamt of using formula, and it is only when a health visitor reassures her that this won't stop me solely breastfeeding in a couple of days that she understands that this is short-term.

I suspect it's also unsettling for all mothers to see their children become parents: it's a shift in role, and in priorities. While I hugely appreciate my mum helping me out, I think it's fair to say that I'm not the most gracious host.

It's when she returns home a few days later, but continues to visit me frequently, almost every day at first, making me cups of tea and showering her granddaughter with love, that our relationship becomes more relaxed. We are at ease with each other, content in our mutual adoration of Astrid.

A combination of love and hormones help me float through the first, sleep-deprived weeks of motherhood. It's magical. I expect to feel the baby blues; the drop in pregnancy hormones that leaves many women emotional a few days after giving birth, but I'm too elated. I feel joyful and relaxed, except when I try to leave the house, which is a huge feat. I have to work out what Astrid might need, which seems to be enough to go on holiday with, and what I might need, which is nothing at all, and then walk very slowly – aware of my stomach healing – using the pram for support. I feel very proud when I manage to get even as far as the park opposite my flat.

*   *   *

I don't doubt that, for people in happy relationships, working out how to look after a child in those first few weeks of parenthood is one of the most wonderful experiences, and it helps to cement them as a team.

Not all relationships are like that, however. And there's something beautifully simple about developing a new relationship with my daughter. I don't need to stay up late to find out how my partner's day has been, so if I'm exhausted, I'll just go to bed. I don't feel any self-imposed pressure to look attractive, so that a partner will want sex with me in the future. And there are no complications from two people having different views as to how to look after a baby – or even to compromise over names.

Even with the happiest of relationships, overtiredness can add strain. I've heard friends utter passive–aggressive 'darlings' to each other through slightly clenched teeth. Instead, I'm simply on my daughter's team.

Late at night though, the responsibility of motherhood makes me worry about dying. Who will look after Astrid if I'm not around? Irrationally, I even put some emergency formula milk in my larder so that she won't go thirsty if someone walks in to find me dead. As if shops would suddenly not exist. I find myself wishing I had a partner, mainly because it doubles Astrid's chances of having an alive parent until adulthood.

Gradually, though, the panic about keeping both of us alive wanes; I stop less frequently while walking the pavements of south-east London to put a hand on Astrid's chest to check that she's still breathing. At night, I still look over at her in the little cot that is tied to my bed, but more in wonder and delight at this perfect, beautiful girl who is my family, than in panic that she might not be doing well.

Sleep deprivation only plays one cruel trick on me. I wake one night thinking I've fallen asleep with Astrid feeding on my chest, but she's not there. I start desperately searching under my duvet, on the floor. Where's my baby? Has she suffocated under the covers? I look over to the cot and she's happily in there, fast asleep. I resolve to try not to fall asleep while breastfeeding, just so that I won't wake up panicked.

I love the stream of visitors who come to welcome Astrid to the world, and they give me a window into life beyond the streets which I pace with my daughter in a sling or pram, and the cafés in my neighbourhood. It's reassuring to hear about other people's lives, and to see my daughter cuddle into their arms.

I get to see which of my parent friends enjoyed the first weeks of having a new baby by their attitudes towards me when they arrive. Those whose faces look concerned, and who ask me how I'm coping and tell me it's all going to get a lot better, are usually scarred from tough times when they were looking after a tiny baby. Those who are excited tend to think back fondly on hours where cuddling is the only important thing.

There is one couple who visit with their son, who is a few weeks older than Astrid. Their battle scars are still fresh. They ask me how I'm getting on, and tell me how tough they've found various moments with a baby.

'I find it easier having her than not,' I say and see my friend look utterly baffled. I don't get a chance to explain that I found things tough when I wanted a baby, so a bit of sleep deprivation is nothing compared with that.

I feel very lucky to have the support of friends who want to make sure I'm doing okay on my own. I'm sure it's why I get so many visitors bringing food and offering to help me out. Even as weeks pass, people still keep coming to meet Astrid. Lucinda, who has offered so much support through miscarriages and my pregnancy, comes laden with toys that her children have outgrown, including a mobile that plays classical music, which she used to lull her children to sleep. My friend Laura visits from Belgium to stay for a few days to make sure I get some time off to have showers. And within a month, my daughter has started to smile.

I'm aware that my introduction to motherhood is unusually blissful. There is no guarantee that getting pregnant very deliberately – whether through a donor or at the end of many years of fertility treatment – means that the trials of post-natal depression will keep at bay, or that a mother will immediately bond with her baby.

My friend Jennifer, who used donor sperm to conceive with her husband Nils after finding out that he was infertile, told me about the birth of her son Alfie. She is a writer, and it came at a time she was under huge pressure to get her first book finished. She felt she wasn't able to dedicate herself to motherhood, or to writing. She didn't feel she was excelling at either. She was very open about how she was feeling to her husband Nils. He was enjoying fatherhood, and he reassured Jennifer that she would grow to love being a mother, and that everything would be fine.

She told me she'd wake up thinking she'd had a nightmare, only to realise that it was her reality. She loved her son, and felt capable as a parent, but wasn't enjoying the experience at all.

She refused to wear the ring her husband bought her to mark her son's birth because of the thoughts she was having. Although she wasn't taking medication, such as antidepressants, to help her mood – and there was no question over whether she was able to look after her son – she remembers it as a horrible time. I feel that her honesty is so helpful for many women who don't understand why they aren't elated when longed-for children, however they are conceived, arrive in their lives.

It wasn't until Alfie was eight months old, and the family went on holiday together, that she started enjoying motherhood.

It took time for her to understand that her life was now different. And she needed to accept that she was not going to be a mother like her own mother – giving up her career to concentrate on raising children. She loves her work and wouldn't enjoy spending a year with a baby, but that doesn't make her a bad mother, simply a different one. 'And now my son gives me wings,' she says.

She loved being a mother more and more until she got to the point that she really wanted a second child. When I meet her, she is pregnant with twins. She has planned a clear four months off work, and knows what motherhood entails, but she is aware that post-natal depression could hit once again. 'Now if I experience this again, I know I will get over it,' she says.

When the couple found out that they were expecting two boys, it took her husband Nils a few hours to be happy. He told Jennifer that he had been thinking that if they'd been expecting girls they would be mini versions of her, and the comparisons would be less obvious.

She says that it's always a reminder to Nils of his infertility when people say how much his son looks like him. Both Alfie and Nils share expressions and mannerisms; her son and mother-in-law share a strong resemblance.

Both she and her husband are very open about their son's biological origins. He's now three and a half and will be taught that he has a mummy, a daddy, and a man who helped them to have me. But, she says, it's very easy to forget his genetics.

She feels, like me, very strongly that it's important that donors are identifiable. She hopes that in France, where she grew up and where sperm donors remain anonymous, the law will change so that people have the right to find out their genetic origins. Nils has concerns that when his son becomes a teenager he will accuse him of not being a real dad. But Jennifer feels that any teenager will say this anyway, regardless of origins. 'This donor will never be a father to my son,' she says. 'But they've helped out – and thank God they did.'

I wonder how many donors are aware, when they hand over their warm sperm samples to nurses in clinics world-wide, the grateful families they're helping. I wonder if the students who answered the adverts for donors that I saw at university in the 1990s realised the service they were doing while wanking for beer money at a time in their lives when infertility was very unlikely to have crossed their minds. I wonder what Astrid's donor felt – if anything – when he passed over the jar to a nurse that to me is the greatest gift because it helped me create my daughter.

10

Watching Astrid Unfurl

As the weeks pass, I watch my baby uncurl and unfurl, and become a sturdier, more smiley creature. It's such a quick process from an entirely dependent newborn to being able to support her neck alone. And as my daughter gains some strength, I start feeling reassured that she can fend for herself a little more – or, at the very least, that if something is wrong she'll scream for help.

I'd taken the donor's description of himself as laid-back with a pinch of salt: no one is going to declare themselves to be neurotic. But I think he was telling the truth as I realise my daughter is taking life completely in her stride, is unfazed by most things, and loves meeting new people.

I spend a large part of each day with her sleeping, cuddled into me. One very good friend, whose daughter is just a few weeks younger than Astrid, finds her daughter will only sleep if she's strapped into a sling with her mother on the move. Eventually, she gets a copy of *War and Peace* on audiobook to accompany her regular walks around the neighbourhood, figuring it's the only time she'll manage to make any headway through such a tome.

I laugh as Astrid starts each day by crinkling her eyes into a giant smile, delighted to wake up to the new world around her. And I cry when I hold her to get her vaccinated and see her eagerness turn to screams as pain is inflicted upon her. I make sure she's facing the nurse so that she doesn't feel that I've betrayed her, but it doesn't make me feel any better. Her eyes, which have been dry, cry real tears of shock. I feel conflicted: I'm doing this to protect my daughter, but causing her such distress feels so cruel. I wonder whether it's any easier for people with partners, they can reassure each other that they're doing what is right for their child's health while feeling guilty about inflicting pain.

While Astrid is good-natured, I feel cautious on her behalf. It takes months for me to take my daughter into central London. Instead, we spend our time at local mother-and-baby groups. I conquer my fear of singing in public and relearn the nursery rhymes of childhood. I sometimes feel self-conscious: what do you do at a singalong baby group when your child falls asleep? I mean, I'm singing 'Row, Row, Row the Boat' for Astrid's benefit, not my own, so can I stop if she's snoozing?

I go to baby massage classes, and love catching up with other new mums who are working it out as they go along. I'm asked by one, 'So who are you angry at? We get to take out our sleep deprivation and frustration on our partners. Who do you get to feel resentful towards?'

I get to grips with baby paraphernalia – how to plug in car seats and construct baby rockers – and I get much better at accepting help from people. Gradually, I make friends with people in the area with babies of a similar age, a group of women all off on maternity leave who are free for coffee and to spend time in parks in a way that most haven't experienced since before starting their careers. I regularly meet up with a couple of the women from my NCT group, who had their babies more than a month before Astrid arrived. It might just be a few weeks, but with children so tiny it's clear that they've spent longer out in the world: they're more alert. We take our blankets and lay them out in a patchwork under the shade of trees in the park, putting our babies down to play beside each other, too young to engage with each other but wide-eyed at the sight of leaves moving in the breeze.

I meet curiously few other single mothers (cynics have told me that will change in a few years), except those who are solo by design. Some of these mums differentiate themselves from single mums by chance – especially those who've had a long journey with fertility problems. One mother, who also had artificial insemination, dropped in, 'I mean, I didn't just get knocked up, I thought about this.'

For the first few months, I feel that Astrid and I are completely tied together. There is no sense of self; instead there's a sense of us. And I don't miss what I've lost, because I can only think about the two of us together. I wonder how this would feel different if I'd been in any of my past relationships. I suspect that I'd have felt pulled in multiple directions. By having no partner to neglect, I'm able to suspend my responsibilities to the rest of the world and focus solely on my daughter. In the first weeks, I don't want any separation between us: I find it distressing to spend time away from Astrid. We spend hours and hours gazing at each other, as I tell her what a wonderful baby she is. I notice when she gains a new expression, and I copy her funny faces. My flat is a tip, the pile of unopened post now looks so ominous that I don't want to tackle it, but nothing can make me stressed: love and breastfeeding hormones are a wonderful mix. It's only once Astrid's lost that complete vulnerability that comes with being a fresh-to-the-world newborn that I can even contemplate myself as a separate person to her.

And then I relish rare moments to myself. My amazing cousin Emma comes down from Edinburgh with her daughter to stay, cuddle Astrid and help out. She looks after Astrid while I go swimming. I love the feeling of freedom as my arms glide through water, rather than holding them wrapped around Astrid as I carry her. I start swimming more regularly, racing out when my mum comes round, remembering and rediscovering the strength in my body which has been fully in service to someone else over the past months. But I don't want to be away for more than an hour, and I'm pleased to come back and become us again.

Maternity leave is a wonderful thing if you're lucky enough to find it enjoyable – and I'm one of the lucky ones. I have friends who've understandably gone back to work after a few months as they find it tough being off with a baby whose babble, while charming, is never going to be intellectually stimulating. I'm the opposite and wish for a lottery win that will allow me a few years. My days are joyful; I feel contented. Not only do I get the pleasure of spending time with my wonderful daughter, but I'm also no longer rushing and dashing around, trying to fill my time so that I don't think too much. The yearning that had been my tinnitus is gone from my life.

I wonder whether the first months of motherhood have come as a surprise to other solo mums. Every solo mum has thought hugely about becoming a parent, it's part of the territory that comes with fertility treatment. For many there's been huge longing, but that doesn't mean that the reality of having a dependent baby isn't a surprise.

While I find carrying my constant companion a pleasure, I often wish for an extra hand so that I can fix Astrid's car seat or haul in shopping along with my daughter (rather than traipsing in and out multiple times because I can't load myself with bags). I've never been the most practical person, and I find that lots of baby gear needs constructing. I'm so thankful when a friend gets excited at the sight of Astrid's new flat-pack cot and offers to help construct it: I don't tell her it's been sitting in my home for weeks, while I've felt too embarrassed, or too proud, or a combination of the two, to ask for help.

This seems to be a theme among solo mums: I suspect we're a proudly independent bunch and feel that asking for help is a sign of weakness. But it's especially important for us all to learn to show that vulnerability; feeling overwhelmed does our children and ourselves no favours. And I don't think the lack of help is unique to solo mums. I learn that many women in couples across the country are bringing up their children alone during the week too, but invisibly.

I once said to a friend, 'But there's no one for me to pass Astrid to when I want to get out of the bath.'

'There was never anyone for me to pass mine to either – my husband's at work at bathtime – I put them down on the floor, or into a rocker, and then got out of the bath myself,' she explains. After that, I love bathing with Astrid and position her carefully on the floor before using my arms to haul my body up and out of the bath, my stomach muscles non-existent.

* * *

The only time I spend more than an hour apart from Astrid is one day in August when I'd arranged to go out for breakfast with Bec, a heavily pregnant friend who lives in Birmingham.

She came down to London for a friend's wedding and is thirty-seven weeks pregnant.

'I think I'm in labour, so I won't be able to make breakfast,' she texts in the morning. 'I'm going to get the train home.'

My mind starts whirring: she probably isn't very far into labour, but no one wants to give birth on a Virgin train (even if 'virgin birth' is a strong headline). I suspect she's probably experiencing Braxton Hicks contractions – her body getting into practice for a long labour in a few weeks' time. Her baby is due three and a half weeks later, and first babies tend to be late – right? I don't want her to miss out on the wedding of two of her closest friends if her contractions are likely to fade in a couple of hours, so I text back saying that I'm more than happy to take her to the local hospital if she just wants them to have a little look at her before she gets her train.

I put towels on my car seat in case her waters break, and, half an hour later, we are in the Maternal Assessment Unit, which I've visited so frequently. She is in early labour, and things are starting to pick up. I might not have had the hippy water birth I had dreamt of, but Bec looks like she might have more chance.

The midwife says she probably has time to get back to Birmingham if she'd rather be there, but Bec says she doesn't really feel like travelling. I'm not surprised; her contractions are now coming every few minutes. She says she wants to come back to mine while she waits for things to accelerate.

By the time we leave the Assessment Unit her contractions are coming thick and fast, and soon after we get back to mine she says she wants to go to the bathroom.

All that I'd learnt from NCT classes and pre-natal hospital classes comes flooding back. I could hear the midwife's voice, saying, 'We tend to get very excited when someone in labour wants to go to the bathroom, it usually means the baby is coming soon.'

I called 111 while Bec is in my bathroom. The operator asks questions. I answer as swiftly as I can.

Then he asks, 'Can you see the baby's head?'

I can't see my friend, she's locked in the bathroom, let alone her baby's head, because I'm not looking at her vagina, so I say no. This, on reflection, is definitely not the correct response. If I'd had a look I think I almost certainly would see her baby's head.

The operator says it's not an emergency, and to wait a while at home. I tell him there isn't time.

I get Bec out of the bathroom and into my lounge. She seems to want to push. I realise that Astrid and I are about to become birth partners. Bec's partner is in the US and there's not going to be time for him to get a flight over. I don't even know whether we have time to get to hospital, but we give it a go: I pull together a little hat, newborn clothes, some jelly babies and Lucozade left over from my recent hospital trip, and bundle Astrid and Bec into the car, while pretending to be relaxed and that we have all the time in the world.

Bec starts making mooing noises. I speed to the hospital, park the car illegally and, with Astrid in a sling and Bec stopping every few minutes to moo against a wall, we make our way to the labour ward. Luckily, I know the way. A midwife we'd seen earlier recognises Bec and rushes her upstairs.

She's taken to be examined by a midwife. Astrid and I join her.

'I like your bumbag,' Bec says to her. She's fully dilated and ready to have her baby. How's she so lucid? I mean, she isn't comfortable during the contractions, but she's handling everything like a pro.

I start sponging her forehead. She takes two quick glugs

of gas and air, and then the midwife tells her to stop so that she can start pushing.

'We can't have your baby in here,' she says. 'There's a risk of infection.'

This might not cast me in a very good light, but I think she means a risk of infection to Astrid, and I really didn't want that.

Luckily, there's an Anthony Nolan nurse (whose job it is to collect unwanted placentas because they can help cure blood cancer) who is free. She sits outside the delivery room and plays with Astrid, who seems to take the whole thing in her stride. I am conscious of being so lucky to have a wonderfully laid-back baby; some mums would have had to have their baby in with them. Perhaps Astrid feels secure back in the place where she first came into the world.

I speak to Bec's parents on the phone to try to get a copy of her hospital notes (she hasn't brought them; it hadn't crossed her mind that she'd have her baby early), and when they say they'll drive home to get them, I gently tell them that there is no need. I say that Bec is doing amazingly well and is about to have her baby. The notes will be too late. They set off from Birmingham to London.

I steel myself for the fact that this baby is a little early and might need some help. Twenty minutes later, my mum arrives at the hospital and takes Astrid to the waiting room. Astrid looks around at everyone, smiling, clapping and trying to get their attention. Sadly, for her, women in labour aren't the most responsive of audiences.

Meanwhile, the midwife tells Bec to push as if she is trying to get out the biggest poo she has done in her life.

Bec asks me to take photos. When I start taking them of her face, she points to her vagina. I catch on camera her baby's head crowning and coming into this world. Of life beginning. It's one of the most incredible moments I've ever observed. Her tiny, little baby girl started breathing immediately, and is put on Bec's chest. She's completely well. I cut the cord.

Once the placenta is delivered, Bec, who is utterly in shock because of the speed it all happened, has a bag of crisps. I hold her tiny baby and can't believe how light she feels. Soon, her parents arrive in London. They're elated to be grandparents and thank me over and over again for being there.

Bec tells me it was perfect, and she couldn't have been with someone more relaxed. It was utterly magical. She comes to stay the following night and we line the babies up next to each other, Ren so tiny and Astrid looking grown-up in comparison.

Her boyfriend arrives a couple of days later on the first flight he could get back from the US. I didn't experience the baby blues after Astrid's birth, but after Bec's baby Ren is born I feel emotional.

Until I'd experienced Ren's birth, I'd been in a blissful state. For the first time in many years I wasn't broody. When I saw pregnant women on the streets, I felt vaguely sorry for them, knowing that they might well be uncomfortable and feel like they were lumbering along the road. I was enjoying the sense of freedom of not carrying a growing baby inside my tummy. But something changed when I witnessed a new life, and the next time I saw a pregnant woman that feeling, which I'd lived with for so many years, was back again. I wanted to do it all over again. Not here, not now, but sometime.

* * *

I sometimes feel a little embarrassed by how much I love motherhood. I feel that many women feel inclined to focus on the downsides, to understandably mourn an independent life that is lost to the needs of little ones. Or, at the very least, like the *Vagina Monologues*, to talk about how boring the first year of being a parent is.

There are many books about motherhood that talk about the loss of one's self, and authors who talk about focusing on their careers over parenting. Doris Lessing is perhaps the most famous. She described young motherhood as 'the Himalayas of tedium' and wrote in her memoir that she committed 'the unforgivable' by leaving her ten-year-old son and six-year-old daughter in 1949, when she moved to London from colonial Rhodesia. In fact, she brought her two-year-old son Peter with her, from her second marriage, and brought him up as a single mother in London, writing five novels and her memoir in the first decade of his life. But many mothers feel a diminishing of who they are when they have children.

That's not how I feel. I love being a mum in a deeply unfashionable way. From the cuddles with a wholly dependent baby to watching my daughter start to discover the world, I don't find it unfulfilling – completely the opposite. It makes my heart sing. I don't know whether being an older mum contributes to that. I'm not missing out on nights out, because most of my friends are in with their children. I've spent so much time with my nephews in the past few years that my weekends are already usually family friendly. Perhaps knowing how close I've come to never experiencing parenthood helps me to feel how precious it is: I know I can't take it for granted, as it could so easily not be something I'd known for myself.

On a night out, a friend of a friend is lamenting how much she's lost. How she and her husband used to look at couples whose relationships were based around chatting about their children, or giving each other instructions, and promise that would never be them.

'Do you ever wonder if you've made a terrible mistake?' she asks me. I really want to sympathise and share her woes, but this is a thought that hasn't crossed my mind. I've made mistakes in my life, but Astrid is the best thing I've ever done.

I don't say this; it would feel unsupportive when she is looking for a kindred spirit. Instead I suggest that perhaps it's a little different for me because I don't have a partner. I haven't experienced a change in the most important relationship in my life in order to have Astrid or any sense of loss; all I've had is a gain. And I do reassure her that I think that lots of people feel the way she does.

Even if they don't ask such fundamental questions, I suspect that many solo mums feel overwhelmed at some point during their child's first months on the planet; I know I found the responsibility of looking after a human life weighed heavily. Even walking up my stairs, Astrid in my arms, I'd concentrate so hard on each step so that I didn't fall and hurt my daughter or accidentally bang her against the bannisters.

I've never thought of myself as someone who loves routine, but I notice Astrid and I gravitating to the same places at the same times each week. On Mondays, I join a group of mothers who take part in a fitness class in one of the parks. I mainly go along to chat to them, and am always quick to suggest a coffee afterwards. It's great to share our experiences of teething, or weaning, or travelling with babies. On a Tuesday morning, we'll go swimming together, which doesn't really involve much swimming but is more singing nursery rhymes and pushing rubber ducks around in the water. Astrid laughs with joy when she sees me submerge my mouth to blow bubbles in the water, and she loves playing with the toys, which must make it feel like bathtime, but on a bigger, more sociable, scale. Then, on Thursdays, we go to the singing group at the local play club, led by a charismatic woman who is perhaps five years older than me but has double my energy, and who has the incredible skill of holding the attention of thirty pre-nursery-aged children. I frequently think that she would be my ideal childminder for Astrid, and I see my daughter entranced by her songs – 'Heads, Shoulders, Knees and Toes', 'See the Little Bunnies Sleeping', all the classics – each week.

But while we love our little routines, I think my favourite time of all is very first thing in the morning as we're waking up. We'll lie in bed together, and I'll point to Astrid's toes and make her giggle, or trace my fingers over her palm while telling her nursery rhymes. We'll rub noses, or she'll tug at my hair and I'll explain that it is hair and she's got some too. We've got the whole day ahead of us for adventures, but the simple contentment in these moments, where there's no sense of time as Astrid wakes up to a world that is still so new to her, is magical.

* * *

There is never a moment when I question my decision to have Astrid, but there are some days that are really hard: when Astrid is unwell and won't sleep and won't stop crying, and I just want her temperature to go down and for her to feel more comfortable, and I can do nothing to help and I'm worrying and I wish there was someone to help me. Or if they aren't going to help, at least they can tell me that I'm doing okay, that I don't need to feel tense as well as worried about my daughter whose sunny character I take so much for granted, and who so alarms me when she is miserable and in pain.

I could call friends, but they have their own responsibilities and may well have been having similar situations with their own children at that same moment. And I could call my mum, who I know would come round if I say it's an emergency. But I want to save the emergency call for if there is a worse time, so instead I tell myself that I'm doing okay and that Astrid will feel better soon.

I wait out her illnesses, tracking them in hours between Calpol and Nurofen doses. They are the hardest times, with the calls to out-of-hours doctors and concerns whether to take her to A&E; the repeated examining of her body for rashes that could be meningitis; the wish that I could make everything better. My love for her makes me so protective – I wish I could take the pain for her.

During those times I remind myself that even if I had a partner, they might be out or working late or away.

However long it takes, Astrid eventually falls asleep and I stroke her forehead and feel lucky that I have the most wonderful girl, and hope that sleep makes her feel better swiftly. If she has a fever, I stay next to her, not wanting her to wake alone and whimpering, which she does when her temperature gets really high.

One night, I feel that her hands are boiling hot, a sure Astrid-fever sign. I take her temperature using a thermometer that gives the figure in green when it's good, grey when it's borderline and then red for taking action. As I see it top 104 degrees – bright red – I feel a sense of panic.

Astrid's in a baby sleeping bag to keep her warm and I take her out and start stripping her down to her nappy. She has a slight rash, but it looks viral and nothing like meningitis, which is my big fear with sudden, high temperatures. I give her medicine to try to reduce her temperature, and momentarily wonder whether to take her to A&E. Erring on the side of caution, we head out to the hospital. We sit in the paediatric waiting room and Astrid starts to wake up properly, delighted that's she up and about in the middle of the night, and even more pleased that she's surrounded by other children. She wants to make friends. Astrid's temperature has reduced with the cocktail of painkillers I've given her by the time we're seen by a triage nurse. She meets my daughter, who is by now full of smiles and immediately starts playing with the Lego brooch the nurse is wearing. A doctor diagnoses a virus and we're sent home pretty speedily.

The next time Astrid's temperature skyrockets I feel a sense of panic, strip her down and decide to just keep an eye on her. My instinct is that it's a virus again. But in the morning her breathing is laboured, so I call 111, who send an ambulance. Astrid's already perkier by the time the paramedics arrived, but they take us to hospital. Again, we're told it's a virus, but I'm given a stern telling off for not taking her in the night before, as alarmingly high temperatures do need medical attention, especially in a child too young to say how they're feeling. I feel dreadful, as if I've let Astrid down. I wish fleetingly that I had a partner so that we could have made a decision together – I feel so responsible. Luckily, Astrid makes a swift recovery, unaware of the guilt I am carrying.

I don't know what I'll do if something truly serious happens.

11

The Gift

As for the donor, it is only once Astrid is a few months old, and I am able to appreciate time on my own, that I look at his picture again, hoping to see if there is a resemblance between the two of them. Perhaps I'm so slow because I know that most babies look like their dads, and I want to feel that she is mine.

By the time I look, her smile is so similar to mine, and I can see me in her through her expressions. I don't feel-threatened by – just grateful to – the amazing mystery man who has helped to create my daughter and bring her into this world.

I find that I'm really pleased to look at the photos of the donor, both as a baby and as an adult. His open, happy baby face definitely shares similarities with Astrid: they both look so excited about the world.

I start feeling curious about him. I have so many details about him that I know that if I were to put them into Google I would be able to find his identity speedily: I have his photo and know his profession, it would be very easy to complete the jigsaw. But if I were to use my googling skills, I don't know how it would affect my relationship with Astrid: I always want to be honest with her, and if I know more about her donor, I'd have to keep something back.

I realise that, for possibly the first time in my life, I'm going to ignore my curiosity. This is Astrid's story as well as my own, it's our family story and we share it – but it's her choice whether she wants to get in touch with her donor when she is eighteen. If she's inherited my insatiable curiosity, and technology continues along the same trajectory, I imagine that by the time she might have any interest in her donor she'll be able to find out all the information she wants just by scanning a picture. But she might be disinterested too: this man is a donor, not a dad. They share DNA, but they don't have a relationship. I'll support her, whatever she chooses.

I get in touch with the sperm bank to ask if I can write a thank-you card, or whether that's inappropriate. They tell me that I can, but only if he asks specifically whether anyone's tried to get in touch with him will it be passed over.

How do I write a card thanking someone for their sperm? It's such a big thing that I'm frozen into inaction. But it's something that I want to do, however inadequate words might be to express thanks for a daughter. I think about it occasionally when Astrid's awake at four in the morning, and forget frequently in the haze of sleepiness, which is a constant during the first six months of life with my daughter.

I decide to write a letter. I want to let the donor know how happy I am, and how happy Astrid is. What a delightful, curious, engaged child she's transforming into, changing by the day as she discovers this wonderful world. I enclose a picture of her. It makes me feel emotional, but also that

I'm doing my best by Astrid: if he does by any chance pick up the letter from me, then he'll perhaps feel some kind of link with her from afar. He doesn't know Astrid, but I hope that it will mean that if she gets in touch when she's eighteen, or older, he will have a recollection that he helped to create her.

I speak to American sociologist, Rene Almeling, Professor of Sociology at Yale University, who has researched how we understand the value of donor eggs and donor sperm. She has found that our attitudes towards gender shape our thinking about donors in so many ways – and it's fascinating. She tells me that sperm donors in the US have to be a minimum of five foot eight inches tall, whereas there's no height minimum for egg donors. We inherit our height from both our biological mother and father, so this is slightly illogical.

She's found that people want an egg donor to be doing it for noble reasons and donating because they want to help people rather than wanting money, despite motivation not showing up in DNA, because there's no known gene for altruism. Whereas women are paid thousands for each egg donation in the US, and men are paid closer to a hundred for a sperm donation, it is the women who are careful to say that they are doing it for the 'right' reasons. I suggest to her that the price difference makes sense, because it's so much more intrusive to donate eggs, but she points out that men donating sperm also have to stick to a healthy regime where they can only have sex at prescribed times. There are fewer egg donors and she believes that culturally giving up eggs is seen as a much bigger sacrifice.

Most striking, though, is the attitude of donors towards the children that they help to create. Dr Almeling has found across her research that egg donors are emphatic that they are not mothers of these children: someone else was pregnant and gave birth. It's the mother who raised the child in every way, from changing nappies to teaching them to be kind. The donor is simply that: someone who gave the possibility of life.

Sperm donors, though, feel that they've given half their genetic material and are in some way fathers.

Dr Almeling believes that the difference is because of the traditional roles of mothers and fathers in society. If egg donors thought of themselves as mothers, they'd be the worst type of maternal figure, giving up their children for a few thousand dollars, so culturally they almost *have* to think of themselves as not being mothers.

We break motherhood into stages: gestation, childbirth, raising children. Whereas a man's role in pregnancy is to provide the sperm, he never gets to feel a baby growing inside him.

Plus, the idea of an absent father already has a cultural acceptance in society, whereas an absent mother is seen as more scandalous.

A US study of donors who have been in contact with their donor-conceived children found that there is a curiosity felt by donors in the years that elapse after they provide sperm.

I want to find out from donors how they feel about these children who are related genetically, but not socially. I'm very aware that the people who are likely to be willing to chat to me are, by their very nature, the ones who are engaged with the role of donor, or they wouldn't think there was anything to talk about.

My friend Tom, who donated sperm to two of his best friends, feels loving towards the children he donated sperm to help create.

Tom is careful not to describe them as his sons, but instead they are his friends' sons that he helped create. But he finds the lack of words for twenty-first-century families frustrating: he is the biological father to the children, but he's not their parent or dad, because, he says, 'Those words are an act, they involve time, money and responsibility. They are the acts of nurturing and providing. That's not me.'

One day, in 2011, he was thinking how exhilarating it is that something can come into your life and turn it upside down, and how, when he was younger, he was so scared of change and tried to keep everything the same. He started shouting in his mind: 'Come into my life, whatever it is, let's go.'

That night, just as he put his head on the pillow, his Blackberry pinged. It was an email entitled 'Don't open this email, it's crazy' from one of his closest friends, Kate.

In it, she said that she and her partner Amy were hoping to start a family and would love him to be part of it by donating his sperm but that they totally understood if he didn't want to. They also made it very clear that they wouldn't be offended at all if he decided, for any reason, that donating wasn't for him.

His gut instinct was yes. But rather than agreeing immediately, the three of them had a series of meals where they talked about all different scenarios and what would happen. The women explained that if they both died, any children would be looked after by Kate's mum, who would become their guardian. Tom looks back now at all their naivety, *without* children it is very hard to predict what life is like *with* them.

The couple then sent Tom an email, which laid out terms. He was to have no claim to any parental rights over any children, and they would not be asking for any money. It was a friendly, well-worded agreement.

He had sexual-health checks, and then Kate told him

that she was tracking her ovulation. She asked him not to ejaculate for four days before she ovulated so that his sperm would be potent. When she had a surge of hormones to let her know she was about to ovulate, he went round to her and Amy's flat in Deansgate in central Manchester, just a couple of miles from Tom's home.

When he arrived, he says that they all seemed bashful and awkward, even though they knew exactly why they were there. They gave him a laptop and a beaker, and explained that Kate would be more fertile if she was turned on, so went to their bedroom. Tom went to the spare room, and ejaculated into the jar, which he handed straight over to his friends.

He stayed the night and the following morning ejaculated again to maximise Kate's chance of getting pregnant.

Six days later she texted Tom saying: 'I just know that I'm pregnant!' Her instinct was correct, and her first son, Luke, was born in hospital nine months later.

Tom says that his world was suspended when he knew that she was in hospital while he waited for news of the birth. He put on a smart shirt, ready to visit, and waited. And waited. He started pacing and couldn't settle, played a game of pool with a friend and kept checking his phone. There was still no news when he went to sleep. Kate nearly died in childbirth, and both she and Amy were too shaken to speak after their son had been born, but they sent a picture. It was five days later that Tom went to visit the family in hospital.

He looked at the tiny baby and had to remind himself where it came from. He doesn't remember it, but he's been told that he said: 'Wow, this is my son.' That night, he felt elated: so full of life. Kate and Amy sent an email a few days later saying how offended they felt by his use of language, but he says it was an involuntary reaction and they have later explained that they were feeling hugely hormonal.

Four years later, after three miscarriages, the couple had their second son, again using Tom's sperm. He saw the toll that the miscarriages took on both Kate and Amy, and was relieved for them when Kate was finally able to carry a pregnancy again.

The boys have always known how they were conceived. Tom remembers being round at their flat when the eldest was two, and Kate opening up an Usborne sex education book. She asked her son what the different body parts are: 'That's a vulva', 'That's a penis', 'Those are testicles', he said.

'And what's in the testicles?' she asked.

'Sperm,' he replied.

'And what did Tom give us?'

'Sperm,' he said.

'And where did it go?' she asked.

'Into Mummy's tummy.'

Seeing this, he felt that their parenting was progressive.

There have been moments when he's angered Kate and Amy. He met a woman at an art fair who was pregnant at the same time as Kate, with a child due roughly the same date. By chance, he bumped into her on the bus several months later and they compared baby pictures of her son and Kate and Amy's son that he helped to make. Later, Tom mentioned this to his friends and they sent him a message saying: 'We're really uncomfortable with you showing photos of our children on public transport.' He says that he knows this makes them great parents, they have a strong instinct to protect their sons.

Sometimes it can be difficult: he feels that his relationship with Kate and Amy is going to continue to evolve over the years. Currently, it feels as if there's a power imbalance: it's not a friendship, but they're not family either – he's not sure what they are.

It can feel like a burden: he has no responsibilities to the family on paper, but he loves all four people in that family unconditionally. He feels that his first lifelong commitment was made to them. Their family is not his life, but it also is. He's not part of the family unit, but in some ways he is. Every time he sees Kate and Amy's sons, his heart melts.

Although he has never regretted for a minute donating to his friends, he wonders sometimes if they would have preferred a donor with whom they weren't so close, and whose life wasn't completely entwined with their own before having children. It now means that he's a huge presence in their lives. But that is exactly why Kate and Amy approached him in the first place: they wanted a donor who would be a magical figure in their children's lives.

He currently teaches Kate and Amy's eldest son football, and they will drop him off ten minutes early so that they can spend a little bit of time together. He looks forward to spending time with the boys as they grow older too.

Tom feels that they're a positive guide in his life. He remembers when he first donated his sperm he was renting a room in a shared house, having just finished a course in audio engineering. He has made a huge success of his career and is sure that it is partly because he was so worried about being a role model. 'Maybe that's why I've worked so hard, as if making money will make me a better biological donor – which, of course, it doesn't,' he says.

He hopes that he'll have some money set aside by the time the boys are eighteen so that he can help fund them through university, or help them travel around the world. 'I'd like to help them,' he says. 'And, of course, that isn't asked of me at all.'

I'm aware that Astrid's donor is very, very unlikely to have given even a fraction as much thought about her life. Asking a close friend is a different way to choose a donor, and I suspect it works well for this trio because Tom never wanted children of his own: I wonder how much more complicated it would be if he were longing for his own family.

* * *

Shortly after chatting to Tom I receive what feels like a body blow. I keep hearing murmurings that the US doesn't have strict regulations with sperm donors; that, unlike the UK where the limit is ten families, over there one man can provide sperm for up to fifty families, so potentially fifty or a hundred or more children.

The UK regulations seem sound. I imagine that the idea of ten or potentially twenty half-siblings could be fascinating; taking into account the fact that many might not be interested in meeting at all, and some might not know their genetic history, this seems a manageable number. Astrid might find it exciting; she may also be completely disinterested – that's something for her to decide and for me to support.

I email the sperm bank in America that has been recommended to me by the clinic in London to check that the legal upper limit of ten families applies to sperm sold to the UK. It seemed clear to me when I was choosing Astrid's donor that many donors weren't eligible for the UK. I received a lovely, reassuring email back:

'You are correct, to comply with UK law there's a maximum of ten families worldwide for the UK donors, I hope that answers your question. Happy Holidays.'

I am so relieved, and I put it to the back on my mind for the next four months. Then, one day, as the thought of donors is uppermost in my mind, I decide to double-check, so I email again, and receive a swift response:

'I'm not sure where 10 families worldwide came from, but reading through the previous email I do not see where it was mentioned. The United Kingdom has a limit of 10 families per donor, but that is only within the United Kingdom. Worldwide a donor may have a total of 60 families . . . With a current world population of 7.2 billion people, 60 does not seem like such a high number—especially considering the UK has a 10 family limit. Please let me know if there are any other questions I may answer for you, apologies for the miscommunication.'

The reply confuses me. It's a direct contradiction to the previous email. The clinic seemed in disbelief that I didn't know this, but then, if their own staff seemed unaware, I couldn't fully blame myself.

As our emails go back and forth, with me increasingly frustrated that they don't seem to acknowledge what serious misinformation I've been given by them, the sperm bank points me to somewhere on the website where the information was shared. How can a country that insists on writing 'Caution – Hot' on coffee containers feel content selling sperm to people in the UK – where the law is different – without making it clear on purchase that there could be so many more families using the sperm?

I send more emails to the sperm bank. I want to protect Astrid more than anything in the world, but I've made a decision that could have a lasting effect on her understanding of family.

I don't know if it's going to upset her to find out how large her biological family is: she might be excited by it; she might be overwhelmed by it. But she's my daughter, and I want to make sure she feels as secure as possible about her place in the world.

I feel strongly that other women should be warned that donors flagged for use in the UK are not limited to ten families worldwide. I speak to a solo mum friend who almost got sperm from the same sperm bank and was equally unaware, and understood the limits as I did. She spent a year researching donors, so I feel that I'm not alone in being confused about this. How had no one mentioned to me that the ten-family rule does not apply, not at the clinic, not the counsellor and not the sperm bank?

My brother sends me a message that helps. He tells me that I'm looking at it through the wrong lenses: Astrid's future happiness is not about the number of genetic half-siblings she has; it's about how I bring her up over the next two decades, about how loved and secure she feels, the relationships she builds. And slowly, I get some perspective. As long as my daughter is healthy and happy and secure, all is good with the world. I breathe.

This is something I would have liked to have been fore-armed about. It feels wrong that it's come as a surprise. I'm glad I chose to triple-check that the email I received was accurate now and not when Astrid was eighteen. She will grow up knowing this information, and for that reason it's unlikely to faze her. I cannot imagine the consequences, because they're in the far future. All I can do is make sure that she's the most loved and secure girl. But I do know that Astrid is who she is because of the donor I picked, so I don't, for even one minute, wish I'd chosen a UK donor, because then my daughter wouldn't be here today.

I want to learn more about donor siblings and whether they frequently lead to meaningful relationships in people's lives so that I can have some insight into how best to intro-duce the subject to Astrid when she's older. I initially set about tracking down some of the Barton Brood – some of the first people to be conceived by a donor – who have found out that they have huge numbers of half-siblings that they were unaware of until adulthood. Perhaps they can help me understand how being from such a massive genetic family could enrich Astrid's life.

The first people I contact don't want to talk about their experiences. But then I get in touch with Janice Stevens Botsford, seventy, an artist and psychotherapist who learnt that she was one of the Barton Brood when she was in her early twenties. Janice and her brother were brought up in England, unaware of their biological origins, until their father died.

Mary Barton and her clinic colleagues told Janice's parents – as they did everyone who needed help getting pregnant – to never disclose the use of a sperm donor to anyone. As for many families, it was only when one parent became so very uncomfortable with the burden of secrecy that they told their children their true genetic origins.

This secrecy couldn't be more different from the family atmosphere between Astrid and me, and it is a reminder to me that society has changed so hugely over the last half-century.

'There are a number of families where it happened in a similar fashion,' Janice says. Some children found their whole identity was disrupted because they didn't know who they were any more; others started to wonder about the role of trust in their family. Although Janice was completely bowled over, she says that her mum explained it in such a loving way that it didn't feel negative or disruptive. I'm touched by how important love and security are in helping people to cope with even the most unexpected of news, but I'm equally relieved that Astrid is growing up in a time when there is more freedom.

Janice's first realisation was that half her genetic background was unknown. She looked at her nose, her chin, and wondered which parts came from her mother, and which from an unknown source. It had never crossed her mind that she wasn't related to her dad. Even though Astrid will always know about her origins, I wonder whether she'll look at herself in the mirror and wonder whether there are any traces of her donor. We look strikingly similar, but she has a more petite nose and chin. I have photos of her donor too, so hopefully the mystery will be reduced, as she can see for herself – although still images never capture the expressions that make up so much of how a person looks.

The discomfort Janice felt at learning something so unusual about herself meant that she left the whole subject buried for years, too complicated to explore. Then, when her daughter was about to be eighteen and Janice was approaching her late forties, she and her brother, Barry Stevens, started to research the identity of their donor. They were both curious. At doctor appointments, Janice was unable to share half her medical history – she didn't know if she might be predisposed to certain hereditary illnesses – and that became another impetus for researching her family.

She found exploring her genetic identity emotional but fascinating. Her brother, Barry, made two documentaries, *BioDad* and *Offspring*, on the subject. The pair found out that they came from different donors, so biologically they are half-siblings, although her parents asked for the same donor to be used. But Janice says: 'Our parents are our parents, my brother Barry is my brother – we'll always be the closest siblings. I've had a relationship with him all my life, and we will till we die. It's unique.' Her words reinforce my understanding that family is primarily about relationships that develop over a lifetime, regardless of biology.

She explains to me how she has met six half-siblings over the past decade. They have become important to her, and her life has been enriched by the warm, welcoming, open relatives she's got to know.

Janice, who now lives in Michigan, was pleased to learn about the donor who helped to create her, and felt sad that he'd died so that she wasn't able to meet him. He was the English neuroscientist Derek Richter, who is considered one of the forefathers of the science of brain chemistry and founded the Mental Health Foundation. She knows he donated to the clinic from 1945 to 1952, and suspects the half-siblings she's met are a few of many children that he biologically fathered, most of whom she will never know.

She's fascinated by what's passed on through generations genetically, and she and her half-siblings frequently talk about nature versus nurture as they're struck by their similarities. Of the seven half-siblings, including her, all are above average intelligence with further degrees; they're all open, curious people who have continued learning throughout their lives, and they are all very active. There's a creative link: they are all artistic, whether painters or musicians, and all have children. Several of the half-siblings have careers in mental health, despite not knowing their biological father's history. Janice has a masters degree in social work and has a psychotherapy practice, while her thirty-seven-year-old daughter is a psychiatrist.

She's joked with her brother, Barry, that some of her group of half-siblings have a preference for tea over coffee, and like to go hiking, whereas a few of his group of twenty-five-and-counting half-siblings are coffee drinkers who have less of an interest in physical activity.

I already see a love of ball games in Astrid that I suspect she hasn't inherited from me, and wonder whether – hopefully – she might find herself being picked for school sports teams: something that eluded me and that she'd have her donor to thank for. She also seems to be less clumsy than I am. My childhood was punctuated by fingers trapped in doors and, while it's perhaps too soon to say, I notice a dexterity in my daughter when I lift her up to use door knockers and see her pulling herself up against furniture that I can't take credit for.

When Janice looks back on her upbringing, she feels that there was a little bit of distance between her and her father, but this could easily be on account of his generation (he was twenty years older than her mother at a time when fathers were a lot more hands-off than today) rather than his feelings surrounding his infertility.

She believes very strongly that offspring have the right to know their biological origins, and says that it was a group of donor-conceived adults from the so-called Barton Brood, alongside the charity Donor Conception Network charity, who put pressure on the UK government to change the law in 2005 to make sure donor anonymity came to an end.

She recommends that parents who have children where a donor is involved let their children know how much they are wanted, which is exactly what her mother did with her. It made it much easier for Janice to come to terms with the news that a donor helped to create her. She suggests that once a child trusts their parent, they can then lead them through knowing about themselves, accepting all parts of themselves, including those that come from the donor. Stability and strength are most important, she feels, so that a child feels supported, that the world is a very safe place, and that they are free to ask all the questions they might wish to. This sounds like great parenting advice: I want to make sure Astrid feels secure enough to have the confidence to explore different parts of her identity in whatever way she would like. I can imagine that I might get in touch with Janice in years to come when Astrid starts asking me questions about donor siblings.

Janice puts me in touch with her half-brother, Alan, who grew up in Hertfordshire. Unlike Janice, he had a sense that there was something wrong as he was growing up. As a teenager, he felt a huge, undecipherable pressure, which he now puts down to the secrecy of his origins.

His mother, who worked as a nurse, read about Mary Barton's clinic in a nursing journal. She had treatment at the clinic and, as with all patients, had to sign a form saying that any child conceived from treatment would never be told about it. After the treatment, she was told, as was standard, to go home and have sex with her husband – meaning that there was always an element of doubt over who fathered her children.

She went to seek support from the Baptist Church, and was told that she'd committed adultery by receiving semen from another man and that any child she carried would be a bastard.

Despite being rebuked by the Church, she wanted a large family and went on to have another child by donor conception. The child died aged seventeen. He was born mentally handicapped and her Church told her that it was a punishment from God.

It feels like the cruellest response to a woman who desperately wants children. And, thankfully, one that wouldn't be acceptable now.

Alan was a fairly stable child until he was fifteen, but in his teenage years he became disturbed, and was prescribed antidepressants to help him cope. When he was seventeen, as part of his biology A level, he and his classmates tested their blood groups. Alan was B positive. At home, he asked his parents their blood groups: his mum was O, and his dad A negative. He told his parents this wasn't possible, and he must have made a mistake in the testing. His father went white and silent: the appalled shock on his face will always be etched on Alan's memory.

Weeks later, Alan had what he describes as a nervous breakdown, and he was referred to a clinic which specialised in teenage psychiatric problems. He was taking antidepressants and tranquillisers, but his therapist said that what he was going through had to be closely connected to the relationship between him and his parents. She asked if his parents would join their next therapy session.

He went home, told his mother what the therapist said and watched her dissolve into tears. She was not usually highly emotionally expressive. She told him, 'I always knew you'd have to know sometime.' And then she revealed the story of his conception.

Alan felt a huge sense of relief, as if a burden he carried had lifted. He'd always sensed something was wrong, but he hadn't known what. It had become a black secret in the life of his family, and he's convinced that it had a negative effect on his mental health. His suffering reminds me how corrosive secrets within families are, even if they're kept with the best of intentions. I feel for his mother, who shouldered so much guilt, and for him as a teenager, not understanding why life with his family was charged with the weight of a dark secret. I'm so glad that donor conception is no longer hushed up.

Alan's relationship with the man he had believed was his biological father was poor; he felt that he wasn't interested in him and preferred being out at work. In contrast, his mother, with whom he was very close, was highly protective of him.

Overnight, he was able to relax into life. He felt as if a

thousand questions he didn't know to ask had been answered. There was no anger, just sweet relief. His mental health became more stable, although he's suffered from depression on and off throughout his life.

His conception remained a huge taboo in his life: until a decade ago, he had only told a couple of girlfriends and his wife about it. Then, in 2009, he read a newspaper article about donor-conceived families. Alan's father had died, so he felt able to find out more – it's something he'd have never explored while his father was alive. He had his DNA tested with the Donor Conceived Register, which helps people find relations. Results came back that his donor was neuroscientist Derek Richter. Alan felt pleased that such an incredible person had helped to give rise to him, and I get the impression that his DNA is something he feels proud of and is a great comfort to him. I wonder whether it is more important to him than Janice, partly because of the distance he felt at home between his father and him while he was growing up.

He was told he had six half-siblings – three of whom are children from Richter's marriage. He gradually got to know them, and no longer feels ashamed and traumatised by his past. He's now open about his history, and he feels so glad to have met such a nice family who he's regularly in touch with. His mother has also met some of his half-siblings, and she is very supportive of him spending time with his biological family: she'd always wanted him to have lots of brothers and sisters, and now he does.

It's a reminder of how important my support – just as Alan's mother gave hers – may be if Astrid chooses to pursue relationships with donor half-siblings. I never want her to feel as if she has to keep any part of her family secret, or separate, in the way that some children feel if their parents are divorced or families have blended. Instead, if she does decide to get in touch with donor siblings when she's older I want her to feel confident that we're all part of one family, however unconventional, all joined through her.

It is now very rare indeed that people hide their children's origins from them if they've been donor conceived, but it does still happen. Some people don't believe that their families or friends would be accepting, or are scared. I suspect that in this day and age it would never remain a secret for long: people's genetic make-up is likely to start influencing medical treatment within the next few decades, and I feel that it is a recipe for children to experience a sense of betrayal.

Soon after I've spoken to the Barton siblings, a friend puts me in touch with Naomi, a solo mum who found out the donor she used had created more half-siblings than she'd initially been aware of. She has had a lot of time to process this information, and I'm interested to find out whether it ever concerns her.

Naomi decided to become a parent as she approached forty. The strong yearning in her mid-thirties turned into an obsession as her milestone birthday drew closer. She started trying to find a co-parent: someone else who really wanted a child, and was happy to take their share of responsibility in raising them, but without the romantic attachment. She was hoping she might meet a new gay best friend, but it was harder than she expected. She didn't feel that trying to become a parent was a choice for her: having a child felt like a biological need. She was losing her mind with the drive to become a parent, she could feel the arms of a baby around her neck, and she didn't feel that she could have lived every day for the rest of her life in that state.

One man – a dentist – had already contacted her on a

co-parenting website offering to be a donor, and she got back in touch and accepted. He knew more than her about women's fertility cycles, and was able to tell her that she would only be able to conceive for 24 hours after she ovulated. When she told him she was ovulating, he jumped on a train from Bournemouth in Dorset to Maidstone in Kent. As she went to collect this complete stranger from the train station – the man she hoped would help create her child – she reflected on how bizarre it all felt. She took him to her house and he produced sperm for her to inseminate. Feeling slightly overwhelmed, she asked what usually happens at this point. The donor – an expert in teeth rather than gynaecology – said that he usually does the insemination, and that it is often more successful this way. So she agreed to let him inseminate her.

He stayed the night, and in the middle of the night he knocked on her door, saying that he had to inseminate her again, because if he did it twice it would be more likely to work. However unsettling Naomi found the whole experience – and, for me, as someone who feels cautious about inviting a date off the Internet to my own home until I've met them a few times, it sounds scary – it was also effective. She became pregnant, and her daughter was born nine months later. Her daughter is now seven, and Naomi believes that she misses not having a father but is very happy. She remembers that one of her first sentences was: 'Where's daddy?' Naomi has always explained the truth, and told her that the donor is a very kind man who helped to make her, but that he can't be a real daddy. I wonder when Astrid will start asking this question. At the time Naomi conceived, the dentist had already donated sperm to make eight other children, and she thought that her insemination would be one of the last. But he went on donating monthly for three more years, countrywide and overseas, and Naomi's daughter now has thirty or forty genetic half-siblings.

He has set up a secret social media page so that the mothers can ensure that none of the related children meet by chance and start a relationship together. It also allows the families of the half-siblings to get together, although, so far, Naomi and her daughter have not been to any meet-ups. This is partly because of timing, but partly because Naomi has some reservations: perhaps her daughter and her half-siblings would find they had little in common, which might be disappointing, or perhaps her daughter would form a very strong attachment to one of her half-siblings, which Naomi would struggle to support as a busy single working parent with no family help.

Although Naomi wasn't aware of the number of genetic half-siblings her daughter would have, she remains grateful to the donor: he helped to create her daughter. She tells her about her half-siblings because she doesn't want her to feel shocked when she's older. She feels it's important that it's normalised.

I agree with her about being open. I want Astrid to know about her genetic half-siblings as she grows up so that it doesn't take her by surprise, in case it has an impact on her identity. But Naomi doesn't seem to find the number of half-siblings especially remarkable and seems far more focused, sensibly, on the two of them as a unit.

She says that there are times when she wishes she had a more conventional family. She's currently got two students staying, and her daughter said to her: 'Why are they coming to stay with us? They're meant to stay with a family and we're not a family, because we don't have a daddy.' Naomi explained that they are a tiny family, but she felt upset by it. Just hearing her talk about it makes me feel sad; I can't imagine how I'd feel if Astrid, unthinkingly, said we weren't a family, though having heard young children ask why their parents are fat, or ask them when they're going to die, I know I may have to brace myself for many a direct question. Naomi reassures me that she's very close to her daughter, who is emotionally well adjusted, but she admits that sometimes it is really hard.

I find that the news that Astrid will have so many half-siblings makes me even more determined to do my very best to make a full sibling for Astrid – not simply because I'd love her to have a brother or sister, but also because I think it's likely to give her good perspective on half-siblings that she hasn't grown up with. If she's living with a sibling, she's hopefully less likely to build up this extended genetic family in her mind into a fantasy of perfect brothers and sisters, when there's no guarantee that they'll want to meet her, or that they'll become close. Many of the only children I know wished for brothers or sisters when they were growing up. If she too wishes for siblings, I feel that it might be confusing for her, because, in a way, that is granted, but it might be a mirage, or a very different adult relationship than siblings who grow up together, argue and learn and laugh together.

Fertility is so hard to predict, though. I know I've been exceptionally lucky to have Astrid and, as every month passes, there's less chance that I'll be able to make her a sister or brother. I don't want to put myself under a level of pressure where, if I can't create her a sibling – which is an outcome I have to consider, as I was told my fertility was very low – I feel like I've failed her. The one thing I learn from this news from the US sperm bank is that however much I, and all parents, want to protect our children from anything in this world that could possibly hurt them, and however careful we are, there will always be something that we haven't anticipated. Our children are about to write their own stories and forge their own paths through life. Along the way, they'll learn that we're all brilliant and fallible, and, most of all, that we love them to distraction. I only hope that Astrid sees a potentially large number of genetic half-siblings as an excellent thing, or an uninteresting thing – but not a troubling thing.

12

My Shifting Identity

I'm struck very quickly by how tribal parenting in the UK is. I'm always suspicious of anyone who is utterly certain about anything – it seems the preserve of politicians whose policies quickly unravel – and it seems funny that it's the things people are the least confident about that they hold the strongest opinions over. Parenting is one of these things. Most people are agreed that love, security and affection are crucial ingredients for children to thrive. But beyond that, no one really knows whether it's better to be a round-the-clock, stay-at-home mother always there for your children, or a working parent who is a role model for having a career. Or whether it's better to put your child's needs first, or whether by putting your own needs first you're then better equipped to offer your child help. People even have strident views on the details: how to persuade a child to sleep well at night; how to wean them on to solids; whether pink needs banishing from girls' wardrobes.

It's a time when women are most in need of support, but

instead, out of uncertainty, usually confident women who are used to having each other's backs through challenges, careers and culture, flock to those who have similar styles of parenting as if it adds credibility.

I've witnessed party mums who want to show that motherhood hasn't changed them, so they talk more about going out than when they took their social life for granted, and staying-in mums who sacrifice all their evenings as they find motherhood too exhausting to contemplate socialising after dark; I've seen laid-back mums who are happy to watch their children hit each other round the head, and anxious mums, who find taking their child to a playground stressful because they worry about accidents. There are mums who talk about their children and mums who won't say a word about their kids because they don't want to be defined as a mother when they've got lots more to them. There are slag-off-the-partner mums, who seem to spend most of their time criticising their child's other parent, and grateful-for-my-partner mums who spend their time talking about what wonderful deed their partner has just done, usually followed by the comment, 'I'll keep him.'

I'm pretty sure that I fit into all of these tribes – except the partner ones – at some time or other. I find that the parents I meet are all pretty wonderful, and what we share – trying to keep our children happy and healthy – is the thing that counts. I'm frequently taken aback by the support I receive from other mothers. On one play date at the house of a mum who lives around the corner from us, Astrid and her daughter ring tinkling bells together while my neighbour listens to me trying to work out how I can juggle my return to work, while at the same time making sure I spend as much time as possible with Astrid. She gives me advice and contact details for people who may be able to help with work projects, and I leave feeling clear-headed. Another mother who lives locally manages to broker such a flexible return to work that I'm inspired.

I'm conscious that my priorities have shifted, as I now see the world through the eyes of a parent. I've made south-east London my home: I'm friends with my neighbours and people on the streets around me. Spending huge amounts of time in the area during maternity leave means that I know more people, especially those with children of a similar age. The area prides itself on its community, and I've always felt welcomed, but especially so since having Astrid.

One neighbour, who my flatmates and I always described as the heart of our community, and who shares my love for campervans, involves me in a local campaign to reduce plastic waste. He coordinates a huge project that involves workshops, lobby groups and schoolchildren making plastic monsters, which are then hung by a local artist in the churchyard underneath a giant fishing net. That Sunday I go to the local church for the plastic-themed service, where I'm told that the vicar is especially proud that she has three non-believers who attend each week. Astrid loves it: songs, people welcoming her, colours everywhere.

I meet the same neighbour's wife, who suggests that their grown-up children are always available for babysitting if I want a night out, and with her living around the corner she can always step in to help if there's an emergency.

Another neighbour, Liz, who used to teach me piano, drops round for tea weekly, and Astrid becomes a huge fan of her visits. I catch up with my next-door neighbour, a film-maker who leaves care packages with hot dinners on my door when Astrid is newborn. Her five-year-old son regularly asks his mum to play at being an alien. Once, when I apologise for not making cake or something to snack on when we're just starting to get to know each other, she says, 'Oh please, let's not get into putting on a show,' and I breathe a sigh of relief.

I meet mothers at the local park, at my buggy-fit class and at play club. Sometimes we just exchange a few words while pushing the swings, but it helps to give me a sense of belonging. I love walking down the street and bumping into people I know by chance. I start to realise that there are some people whose patterns echo my own, and I see them all the time, and others whose children's naps don't coincide with Astrid's and are out of time with us, so we won't cross paths in months unless by design.

I'm lucky that many of my close friends have had children before me, so they can answer my questions about moving on from bottles to cups, or reassure me when I'm concerned that Astrid isn't putting on much weight. I get a sense that they're looking out for me. I'm able to meet up at the last minute with those living just a mile or two away, reminding me of the village I grew up in where friends didn't need to make plans hugely in advance but would meet up whenever we were free. We spend a lot of time in local playgrounds. My school friends have all left London for Hertfordshire, so we go and stay with them regularly, and they travel down to give Astrid hugs, their older children looking after her as she looks at them in awe. She feels the same admiration towards her older cousins, watching everything they do and following after them.

As a new-to-the-role mother, I find that London itself doesn't feel such a friendly place. Astrid's breathing always sounds as if it takes an effort, and I am concerned about the effect of pollution on her lungs.

I avoid Oxford Street: I read that walking along that road, where the buildings are stained black from the buses, is the equivalent of smoking a cigarette. And I can't work out why bus exhausts are at buggy height just so that they belch into babies' faces; it seems like a serious design flaw.

These are things that don't seem to worry some parents at all, and I do know that I'm very protective of my daughter. One day, when Astrid is almost nine months old, I invite some family friends round for drinks at mine, including their elderly parents. I'm offering bites to eat when I catch one of the elderly parents giving Astrid champagne to drink. I'm furious. I spring forward.

'You can't give her champagne!' I shout.

'Don't be ridiculous, you're overreacting,' she replies. Her generation may have doused their baby's bottles with whisky to get them to sleep, but it isn't how I get my daughter to snooze. I think I'm particularly affronted because I don't have to compromise on how I bring Astrid up because I have no partner who might have different views to me, so it takes me aback that someone would make a decision like this on my behalf, without thinking to ask if I mind. I'm aware that I'm acting as if someone has abused my child, but that's how it feels. All my protective instincts have been sent into overdrive. I spend the rest of the afternoon trying to calm myself down, just wishing I could shut my front door to the world and cuddle my daughter.

My concerns about pollution are more persistent, and less a flare of rage. I know people who have stopped using plastic, or any shop-bought detergents, after having a baby. Perhaps wanting to avoid pollution is my lioness instinct over my cub, and in a few years I'll feel more relaxed about it. But for now, I understand the exodus of parents from the capital. I crave sea air, the smell of ozone on the water, and wish that my daughter will grow up in a place that isn't so thick with pollution that it takes years off people's life expectancies. I can't afford to lose any years to the city; I want to see how Astrid makes her way through this wonderful world.

I hope to swap Tubes, which Astrid and I avoid at rush hour because they're so crammed, for a garden. Then, when she's walking, Astrid can scamper inside and outside, and follow in my muddy childhood footsteps. Growing up in Woodborough, a village in north Nottingham, my brother and I spent our childhood playing in a hollow tree that had been hit by lightning, wading through streams (that ran through many people's back gardens) pretending to be the Borrowers, playing on hay bales and running through the farmer's fields. I'm not sure I can offer Astrid such a rural childhood, but hopefully in the future she'll get the chance to traipse mud into the kitchen.

I'd always presumed my flat was very family friendly. Little did I know that steps up to a front door are back-breaking rather than welcoming with a baby in tow, and that not parking close to my flat was going to make shopping, plus a baby, tricky in the extreme. These are hurdles that most parents have to navigate to an extent, because much of parenting in a couple is a tag-team effort rather than a constant partnership. The main difference, perhaps, is that solo mums can't readily take time out and tag a partner back in.

Whereas I spend spare moments while Astrid's napping gazing at houses online that I could exchange my flat for, a friend with three children has the opposite daydream and finds herself looking at one-bedroom bachelor pads where she could sneak away for silence, alone.

I start considering areas to move to within commuting distance for work, but which would also offer us both a sea-air lifestyle. My daughter may not grow up somewhere with surf, but the sea seems like a good first step. I'm conscious of finding somewhere that is liberal: I don't mind for me, as I'm sure I'll find like-minded souls wherever I go, but when Astrid starts school I want her to feel confident about having a mum and not a dad. A friend of mine, whose mum came out when she was growing up, remembers not being allowed to play at some people's houses because of classmates' parents disapproving of her family. While I can't imagine that happening now, I don't want to take it for granted that I'm likely to bump into solo mums across the country in the same way that has happened in south London.

Another change is the way I approach holidays. A backpack and a flight to a long-haul destination with inviting water somehow isn't so appealing with a babe-in-arms. Nor is roughing it, or not booking accommodation in advance. But the worst of all of these, which I experienced on a weekend away with friends, is noisy rooms: I don't get enough sleep to add in people snoring or partying without wanting to weep. My ideal holiday now involves other children so that Astrid can play, and other adults who are either friends or friendly.

The first time Astrid and I go away together for more than a couple of nights is to Cornwall with my sister-in-law, Jess, her parents and my nephews. Astrid so admires her older cousins and finds watching them play absorbing. I get to take long baths, and Jess's family give Astrid and me the most comfortable bed in the cottage. Maybe it's the sea air for Astrid, maybe it's the Cornish cider for me, but we both sleep well all week.

Our first trip abroad is to Ibiza. I'm offered a work trip of a lifetime (especially appreciated during my frugal maternity leave) and we head to the world's party capital to find seclusion and tranquillity at a yoga retreat aimed at mothers and their young children. People warn me before I go that there's no switching off on holiday as a parent: it's just a case of being a mum in a different location. Here, I am given a chance to remember myself.

While I go to morning yoga classes, Astrid, now six months, is looked after by childminders. There are a dozen children on the retreat, from three months old to three years, and it's the first time that anyone apart from my family has looked after Astrid. During the first class I strain to try to hear my daughter, worried that she might be distressed. This is no way to unwind: by the time the class ends I'm stressed and wound up. Then I catch up with the childminders who show me photos of Astrid playing with the other babies, and tell me that she's enjoying herself. I realise she's in excellent hands.

I begin to love the luxury of concentrating on myself for a couple of hours each morning for the first time since I was pregnant, knowing that Astrid is having a good time too. And I feel that I'm a better mum to her afterwards, as I feel refreshed – a sensation I thought I'd experience again in a couple of decades.

I bumped into friends with a son Astrid's age, by chance, on the flight out to Ibiza, and we meet up one afternoon of our holiday. The babies have a picnic and Astrid takes her first dip in the sea.

Each evening at the villa everyone on the yoga retreat shares a vegetarian feast – Astrid trying different flavours and decorating the terraces of the villa with vegetables. And then, once our children fall asleep, we creep down to the kitchen for a glass of wine. I love getting to know this wonderful group of women who share their parenting experiences and tell me how they navigated returning to work. We are all open and supportive of one another, and by the end of the week we make plans to meet up.

Astrid loves her holiday too; she appreciates the company of all the children, particularly a three-year-old girl who she's enchanted by and who plays with her constantly.

On our last morning, we sit in a circle on the terrace to end the retreat formally. We each pass a wish to another woman, sealed with a string of Mala beads. 'With these beads, I give you the gift of joy,' Nina, one of the guests with a daughter the same age as Astrid, says to me. I feel my eyes fill with tears. I pass on the gift of courage. I am struck by how moving these simple, sincere gestures are – and how I feel that I have space to appreciate them. I didn't expect to have time to engage with my inner hippy as a solo mum. We must be the only group leaving Ibiza more rested than we arrived.

*   *   *

As the months pass and I see Astrid growing and learning, and changing and discovering, I reflect upon how unengaged I am with the outside world. I started my career working in newspapers, starting in the most junior role as an editorial assistant. I'd open the post bag and sort people's mail, check through emails being sent in with stories, I would send faxes, book travel and, when I was lucky, research or write stories.

I loved the hum of the news desk, the change in atmosphere during the day as everyone's focus intensified the closer they got to the deadline. I loved the eccentric characters in the newsroom: the reporter who left every day for a long lunch and returned so late that there would be occasional sweepstakes on what time he'd make it back into the office, but he always came back with a story; the writer who told me one Christmas party that he'd done three things he hadn't done in a decade during the last week – a line of cocaine, taken the Tube and hopped on a bus; the editor who internalised stress so effectively that only a twitch in his jaw betrayed when he was feeling under pressure. I learnt so much from the environment, and while the newspaper industry suffered from being hugely late to realise the importance of online news, I hoped to keep writing for newspapers in some capacity in their print form while they still existed.

Later, I worked from Paris in other communications industries, developing strategies for brands and writing their copy, which I also love, but I always kept my ties with newspapers. When I went off on maternity leave, I'd been working as a news editor for the *i* newspaper. Most of the day would be spent working out what stories would go into the paper, commissioning writers to tell these tales and editing their words. I'd keep up with the news, in detail.

I found that having a baby entirely changed my relationship to current affairs. I felt sensitised. Keeping up with what was going on in the world felt painful – I wanted to skip over relentlessly upsetting news, the tragedies that strike every day. Something that I'd have previously found moving would now bring tears to my eyes, and something that would have had me in tears before children was now to be strictly avoided.

I feel concerned for my future working as a news editor: I don't want to go to work to weep at my desk. I'm also conscious that the final running order of daily newspapers is agreed late in the day, simply because of the nature of news and stories developing, so it might feel unsatisfying to leave each afternoon with a sense that the job is still far from complete, particularly given that the role of a parent is never complete either. I know that I'm fortunate that the newspaper's editor supports flexible working so leaving before five to cross London is something I can contemplate.

But while I used to tune in to the ten o'clock news, this now feels late – why would anyone still be awake at ten o'clock when there's a chance that they might be up two or three times in the night?

I start investigating if there are other newspaper roles that I could focus on, or whether perhaps I would be better to concentrate on copywriting work for consumer brands and technology companies where I can fit motherhood around my career.

I think that all parents give consideration to their return to work after having a baby. Childcare in the UK is prohibitively expensive: many women simply cannot afford to go back to work. I join in conversations at my local play club in London with other parents who have children of a similar age. We share our frustrations at the outdated system where women pay the most at a time when they can least afford it, which can feel like women are being encouraged to halt their careers. We talk of promised lands such as Berlin, where nursery is free, just like schools, and countries such as France and the Scandinavian peninsula where childcare doesn't eat the lion's share of an average salary. We look at cultures where it's considered absolutely standard for mothers to finish work early to pick up their children, and where the choice to work or not is simply a preference, rather than a loaded decision that seems to encourage maternal guilt, whatever the best answer for each family might be.

I only hope that when Astrid is an adult, our society will have moved on, and she and her contemporaries won't suffer any maternal work-related angst.

I suspect that solo mums, especially, spend time considering their career after having a baby, as they are both the sole carer and the sole provider in their family. It's something that weighs heavily on my mind. As Astrid's sole parent I want to be there to read her a bedtime story every night and to make sure that I'm there cheering her on at nursery and school events as she gets older. But I also feel more ambitious than before she was in my world: I want to ensure that I can provide for her and that I'm not worried by money. I'm sure that more workplaces are going to become increasingly flexible in the future – thankfully, some are already – it's the only way that parents will feel that they're doing well as both a carer and an employee, rather than never enough.

I chat about my concerns to Kim, another solo mum, who has a five-month-old son and lives in Eltham in South London. She's a few months older than me, and works as a partner in a big law firm. Her mum presumed she was so focused on her career that she wasn't interested in having children. Kim broke up from a serious relationship when she was thirty-eight, after being together with her ex-partner for almost three years. Although she met someone else very swiftly, she realised that her mindset wasn't right to have a relationship: her focus was on having a child, and she didn't want to jump into something serious just to have children.

When she saw an advert on the Tube for London's Women's Clinic she booked an appointment to talk about freezing eggs and buying herself more time. But she was told that at her age there was little point in freezing eggs. The doctor asked whether she'd considered going it alone with a donor.

She went to a workshop held by the Donor Conception Network, and as she was sitting in a room with fifteen other women who were smart, funny and successful, she realised that this was a choice that was open to her.

Her main concern was whether it is fair bringing a child into the world when they will never know their biological father. It's something that I worry about intermittently and was especially concerned about when I was pregnant.

Kim picked a donor through the London Sperm Bank and has very little information about him. She doesn't want to personalise him, or know lots of details about him, but feels strongly that her son can find out about the donor at eighteen, and discover his history.

She spent a lot of time researching her decision, and ultimately thought that she'd regret this forever if she didn't try to have a child.

'Most of my life I've done the normal thing, and this isn't Plan A,' she tells me. 'But I'm really pleased with the way this has worked out.' She didn't tell anyone what she was hoping to do until she was pregnant – not her parents, nor her best friends – except for three women she met at the workshop. She was really concerned that people would judge her, and she didn't want to see their reactions because she wanted it to be her decision.

Once she was publicly pregnant, Kim was amazed at how positive and supportive everyone was. Her dad hugged her and said he didn't want her to miss out on having a child, and her mum was surprised that her daughter wasn't as career focused as she'd believed.

She found the first month of being a mother tough. Her son lost a lot of weight, her scar from an emergency C-section got infected. Her parents had planned to stay for a week and ended up staying for six, by which point she had almost recovered. During those weeks she never doubted her decision, she just knew she needed to get through it.

She was shocked by the sheer responsibility of being a parent, and wondered what would happen if she screwed it up. But this is something that all parents feel, regardless of how many parents are in the mix.

She sees a lot of benefits to being without a partner now: she enjoys making decisions alone and feels that trying to keep someone happy would be a nightmare when she's also got a child who needs her attention. But when her son is sick, she'd love support and someone who cares about him and feels the same way that she does. And she worries that there are things that she knows little about, such as how children stay safe on the Internet, that a partner would be able to help out with and they would be able to talk through together.

'I'd have rather have done this with a partner, but there are definitely positives,' Kim says.

She's been trying to make the most of her nine months off work. She spends a lot of time with solo mums and local mums, but her return to work is also on her mind. She doesn't think her role is realistic part-time. While she's not looking forward to seeing her son only at weekends, she's aware that she couldn't give up work and look after her son all day every day. She feels she needs something else in life, and believes that it will be really good for him to go to nursery. She hasn't ruled out returning to work for three or four days a week, which is her ideal. But although she knows that the other partners within her firm would be supportive of any flexible working requests – diversity and flexibility are massive for her firm – she suspects she would find her job more stressful if she were working part-time. I don't ask her whether she's considered changing roles, because it's clear she finds her work fulfilling and wouldn't want to compromise.

Kim hopes to make a sibling for her son, so she anticipates going through IVF again when he's a bit older. She tells me that if someone had told her four years ago that she was going to become a solo mum, she'd never have believed them. She's proud of herself for taking control and saying that this is what she really wants, and it's important to her. It's by far the best thing she's ever done.

In contrast, Anna, whose daughter is now three, changed career completely to fit around her daughter. She says that it's taken her a while to get to the point where she feels her work is balanced with making time for her daughter.

She moved from London to Salisbury when she was thirty-six weeks pregnant so that she could be close to her family and afford a better standard of living. She worked as a primary-school teacher and, when her daughter was nine months old, she went back to work, teaching a reception class at a lovely school with a great head teacher. She was teaching four days a week and working on teaching admin for another day and a half, but she still felt as if she was falling behind. And if she kept up with it all, she didn't have the energy for anything else.

Anna, who's now forty-one, found the situation was making her unhappy. It had been so hard for her to have her daughter, and she wanted to appreciate her. It didn't make sense to bust a gut looking after other people's kids, while paying for her own child to be looked after by someone else, so she started working as a teacher-led childminder instead. She started off looking after children for four days a week, which she's recently reduced to three days. She loves the flexibility and caring for the children.

Anna was worried about moving out of London in case people's attitudes were less open to different family set-ups than she'd taken for granted. But she's been delighted to meet a handful of solo-mum families. And she loves the lifestyle, with a local school that her daughter will be able to walk to.

She also has a lot of contact with other solo mums, because she set up a secret support group on social media two years ago, which is now used by hundreds of mums of donor-conceived children. It's somewhere that she − and others – can talk about the joys and frustrations of being a lone parent. Mothers share proud, and moving, and annoying moments of bringing up a child alone (both from their challenging children, and the slightly grating comments of friends who say they know what parenting alone is like because their partner works away). It's also a space where they know that no one will come out with the frustrating line, 'But you chose to have them.'

I join this group and find it reassuring, positive and welcoming. I love that it feels like a celebration of all the joys, trials and tribulations of being a solo mum. There's a sense of pride that we've all chosen to be parents, an openness from shared circumstances and a freedom for people to say if they're finding it hard. I've used it to ask people's opinions on moving home, as my decision centres on Astrid's well-being and how important it is to have a support group close by. I also love it when I meet women who post on this group at solo-mum events, as I feel that we have something in common.

We're able to talk honestly, and I feel that I learn a lot from their conversations about talking to teachers at school about their child, or about children being donor conceived and whether they are trying to contact other parents who've used the same donor or are waiting until their children are older.

Anna used to dread Christmas without being in a relationship, tagging along with other people's plans. Now she feels that she's found her tribe: she goes away for New Year with some of her closest friends, who are also solo mums, and her daughter loves playing with their children. She feels that these relationships – that are more than friendships – are really important as the children become almost-cousins. Building a network of supportive solo mums has been crucial to her since having her daughter: there's easy common ground among people who simply understand a shared experience. I hope that Astrid will have a group of such close friends as she's growing up, made up of her cousins and friends' children, and hopefully of children of solo mums too, so she always has a deep sense of belonging.

While I don't know nearly as many solo mums as Anna, she's so right: there's so much common ground and it's a sweet relief to be able to share experiences with people in a similar situation.

* * *

It's not just the question of returning to work that weighs heavily on my mind as Astrid approaches her first birthday, it's also sorting out childcare. I don't feel relaxed about leaving her with anyone else for even part of the week, partly because I know I'll miss her hugely, but also – and this isn't a good reason – because I know they won't love her like I do. I'm pleased to find a nursery for her in a converted Victorian house, which reminds me of the welcoming atmosphere of my primary school. I feel a melancholy that we won't get to spend all our time together any longer, even though she'll get to make friends, play with paints and semolina, and learn to love other adults and children. It's the first stage of letting go, perhaps. It's not comparable to going to school, or leaving home, but it still feels like a shift.

Somehow, even if I did have the funds to delay my return to work, it feels as if there's a world of difference between being a stay-at-home mum with a partner and a stay-at-home mum on your own. The first is a lifestyle choice, the latter simply being unemployed. Perhaps if I were a highly successful businesswoman, or a lottery winner, I'd feel differently.

I am excited to learn what Astrid is interested in when I'm not around; who she makes friends with (as much as an eleven-month-old does make friends) and what she's drawn to discover and play with. My main concern is that my very easy-going, laid-back daughter might be overlooked: she cries rarely and seems to take the world in her stride, and I am worried that other children who are more demanding might get more stimulation and attention. But her nursery key worker is lovely, and I feel that Astrid's in good hands.

I wonder if I'd have found it an easier decision if I had a partner to talk it through with, and consider childminding or nanny sharing. Then I realise how important it is that I have faith in my decisions. I think all parents could freeze in indecision, not wanting to make any mistakes on behalf of their children, and end up doing nothing at all. Really, we're all doing our best.

As I fill in the nursery forms to enrol her, I write in capital letters – where her father's details are asked for – that she was born using donor sperm and I'm a solo mum. I explain to the kind, elderly woman who showed us around that I want people to know in case they make Father's Day cards or there are questions about her having a dad.

'If, when she's older, she says she doesn't have a father, it's not that he's dead or we're divorced,' I tell her, explaining about donors and how very wanted she is.

'Don't worry,' she says. 'There's one child here who has two mums.' I love that she's trying to reassure me, and she describes this lesbian couple with such reverence that it's endearing.

I'm the one who suffers from separation anxiety after settling my daughter in to nursery, and dropping her off for three days a week.

Initially, Astrid cries for the first couple of minutes after I leave, and then I'm told doesn't cry all day, unless she wants milk. But I'm left with the image of her face turning to worry and tears, and it overshadows my day – even if I know she's having a fun time.

But there are glimmers of loveliness. I'm used to spending all my time with Astrid; the responsibility is squarely on my shoulders. And, for the first time, I have freedom to do as I please. I make sure that during her first weeks at nursery, while she's settling in and I'm not back in an office, I sit and read a book. It feels completely alien. Any time I've left Astrid with my mum, brother or sister-in-law has been for a specific reason: I've either been rushing out to meet friends, or for work.

I grow to love that the nursery addresses me as mummy. No one knows my name, but they all know Astrid's. The focus is completely on her, and I'm just her parent. The nursery staff tell me that she's tough, and even if she falls or is jostled by a boisterous classmate she never complains.

Some days, I'm sent a picture of Astrid playing with multi-coloured spaghetti, practising stacking, or playing pass the ball with one of her pals. Friends who employ dog minders to look after their pets during the day receive similar photo diaries, though with more tail wagging. I love these pictures, a tiny insight into my daughter's world when I'm not around.

13

The Big Questions

A baby's first word is traditionally 'dada'. I wonder whether in centuries gone by a father heard his baby's first word and said, 'Yes, child, you are talking about me,' and claimed it for himself, or whether a mother – perhaps trying to encourage her partner – heard the noise and cannily said, 'This is our child's name for you. Now, please change a nappy.'

Astrid is no exception, 'da' has been tripping off her tongue for months. Initially I felt a little self-conscious echoing her babble, saying: 'Yes, dada, that's right,' when there isn't a dad figure in her life. But it soon became part of our patter, and I'd vary it with 'duck' and 'dog' and 'that'.

On occasions though, it has led to others feeling awkward. Astrid was in hospital a couple of months ago, babbling to the young doctor examining her: 'dadada'. 'Yes, your daddy's at home,' he says, trying to make conversation with her. My brain whirs, if I don't say anything it could lead to tricky medical questions further down the line, so I gently speak up, telling him that I am a solo mum but that doesn't stop Astrid saying da all the time. I see him blush. 'I really shouldn't have said that,' he said. I reassure him that I make identical assumptions myself and that he mustn't worry about it.

A couple of weeks afterwards, a heavily pregnant friend-of-a-friend comes to pick up a baby cot that Astrid has now grown out of. I carry Astrid outside to her car, and she launches into her friendly 'dadada' babble. 'Where is your daddy?' the pregnant friend-of-a-friend asks.

I consider whether to leave the question hanging, but that feels a little odd. Instead, I say to her that she shouldn't be offended if her baby starts saying dada before mastering mama, offering Astrid as strong evidence that it isn't personal but just language acquisition. I'd hoped to save her from feeling awkward, but she looked really embarrassed.

It is months later, as Astrid is approaching her first birthday, that she comes out with her first 'ma' sound. I'm putting on make-up, not giving her any attention, and I think the sound was borne out of frustration. 'Mamama!' she said. I was overwhelmed, so much so that I had to reapply my make-up, as tears smudged my mascara.

As for Astrid's actual dada, she is too young to ask questions. I have several books that teach her about different types of family, and how it's possible to make a baby with my egg and sperm from a donor rather than a dad, but I don't think she understands: I just want to get comfortable with chatting about it. Until my nephews ask why Astrid hasn't got a daddy, she's the only person who I've got to practise on.

I really want to know what I can expect, so I meet up for lunch with a London-based solo mum, Christelle, who has just turned fifty and has a seven-year-old son, Etienne.

It was when she was in her late thirties that she felt the tug to have a child. By the time she was forty, she realised she didn't have time to play with. She went online and found many people offering to donate sperm. She created a questionnaire that she asked them to fill in, and chose her donor that way. She thought he was lovely, not her type sexually but wonderful as a father. He wanted more children, his wife didn't and he'd talked to his wife about becoming a donor instead.

For two years, Christelle would time her ovulation using sticks that monitor hormone changes in urine. Each month, she would meet the donor at Paddington train station at the time when she was ovulating. (During several chats with donors and recipients which touch on the subject, I'm surprised by how much sperm donation seems to go on in railway-station toilets.) He'd go to the men's loos and then they'd meet outside, where he'd pass over the warm sperm to her in a pot. She'd go into the women's loos and insert the sperm into her vagina. But, for whatever reason, it was unsuccessful, and so she followed the medical route through a fertility clinic. First, she tried artificial insemination: it worked and she became pregnant, but then she miscarried. She tried again and it didn't work, so then she had IVF, which did work.

When Etienne was three, he started to ask questions about his family. The first was: 'Do I have a dad?' Christelle explained to him that he does, but that he's a donor and he's not in their life. He then asked, 'Does he love me and does he know I exist?'

Christelle says that at this point, her heart broke. She explained that he does know that there's been a baby, but he doesn't know Etienne so he can't love him, but that she loves him very much. It's good to hear how she reacted to this. I can imagine that it could silence me if I was taken off guard. I want to feel prepared so that when – and it is a when, not an if – Astrid asks me these questions, I can respond in the best way to make her feel secure and loved. Whether she makes requests for a daddy, or asks why she doesn't get one while some of her classmates do, I want to be honest in my explanation and to give time to ask her how this makes her feel.

At first, Etienne brought the subject of daddies and donors up every few months, and Christelle would go through the story again, so I expect that Astrid will take some time to work out her family in her mind. And while we chat about it now so that there will be some familiarity, it's currently just words, not loaded with any meaning.

'Now he hasn't asked for a very long time. It's just one of those things for him,' Christelle says.

If people ask Etienne about his dad, he's very confident and comfortable, and simply tells them that he doesn't have a dad.

She has always been open about what she's done: if she meets someone at a playground or in a park and gets chatting to them, she'll tell them. Because she's from the east of France, she finds she's frequently asked whether Etienne's dad is French or English, and she replies saying there isn't a dad but there's a sperm donor. She doesn't want to say there's no dad, in case people think there's a tragedy and it's a sensitive topic. Etienne's school knows his background; Christelle's work colleagues know; people they meet on the street and chat to know. And Christelle thinks that Etienne has picked up that openness, and that's part of why he's so confident. I understand her openness; I feel that secrets – unless they're for surprise parties or proposals – tend to be things that people are ashamed of. And choosing to have a child is something of which we should feel proud.

She has never been on the receiving end of any negative comments, and her parents, who come from a small town near the Swiss Alps, were so welcoming of her choice that the only question they asked was why she didn't do it sooner. They adore their grandson. And she welcomes people's curiosity.

When Etienne was in reception class at school a mum took Christelle aside to tell her that Etienne had told her daughter that he was made in a machine. She replied: 'That's mainly wrong, but not entirely wrong.' She feels that if she doesn't make a big deal out of it, nor will anyone else. And if they disagree with it as a lifestyle choice, they won't say so to her, and it is their problem.

Christelle never expected Etienne to ask her questions about having a daddy when he was so young. And she warns me to expect questions at the least appropriate moments: it is never when you're relaxed at home, she says, but usually in a crowded place when you're in a rush. Etienne first asked when they were leaving nursery, as she was battling to unlock her bike. This feels like all the more reason to prepare myself now and ensure that my responses encourage Astrid to ask any questions she may have rather than accidentally shut down something important to her identity.

He's asked for a brother or sister, and Christelle is blunt in telling him that it's not going to happen. She feels that one child is enough for her. But he has lots of only children as friends, and mostly he's happy not to have to share his mum. If anything, she worries sometimes that they're too close, as they spend all their time together: Etienne has recently started asking her how her day has been when she's been to work, which slightly takes her aback each time he enquires.

Christelle tells me it's only now her son is seven that she's slowly recovering her sense of self. She feels that life narrows when people have children, but even more so for solo parents. There is some truth to this: we lose our freedom in the evenings in the way that people who share responsibilities don't need to. She sometimes feels resentful of people who can go out for a drink whenever they want to. And she's had to learn not to roll her eyes when people in relationships, whose husbands go away for the weekend, say: 'I know what it's like to be a solo mum.' Instead she smiles and nods her head.

Like so many solo mums I speak to, she feels a pang because she'd love to share magical times as Etienne grows up with someone; the milestones such as his first steps, the funny things he does. But she doesn't feel his conception is a huge part of his life: it's how he was conceived, rather than who he is. Just as 'drunken one-night stand' wouldn't define a child, nor should donor conception.

Her bilingual son is from two cultures, and this is how he defines himself, whereas his conception is just part of his history, a moment in time. At his school some children have two dads, others live with their grandma, so he has met diverse families, even if the majority conform to the traditional two-parent–two-children set-up.

Christelle loves her time alone when her son's in bed in the evening, and she's not looking for a partner, though she would like a lover. Big decisions, such as which school to send her son to, can be excruciating for her, but she asks every-body's opinion, treats all her friends as a sounding board, and finds other people's points of view help to inform her own. She asks for help and advice along the way, which requires a level of confidence she believes all solo mums have after some time: some have it innately and others learn along the way.

Sometimes, she feels that Etienne gets a bad deal because she is both a mother and a father rolled into one. She's explained to him before that she doesn't want to be the bad guy, but she doesn't have anyone else. She finds it hard to be both good cop and bad cop, and thinks Etienne also finds it tough. He tells her she is too strict, and while she doesn't think she is any stricter than an average parent, because there's only one of her, it might look so to him.

Although she worries about day-to-day parenting, her private worry is one I think that all single parents share: what will happen when we're not there. It's not something to ever share with a child – unless the worst happens – but Christelle is fostering confidence in her son so that he is outgoing and happy to approach people and start a conversation with them. She feels that this is the best way to equip him with the skills to navigate the world. I think she's very wise; this is all anyone can do.

Christelle says that she was prepared physically for motherhood but didn't realise that being a parent would involve having a child almost constantly on her mind, with only very small pockets of time to herself.

Etienne already has his seven-year-old heart set on growing up to become a dad of four children: Christelle just hopes she is around to see whether his dream changes as he grows older.

While Etienne accepts having one parent who fills both traditional roles of mother and father as best she can, it's possible that he might have more questions as he grows older. But with Christelle's warmth and openness, I feel they'll both take everything in their stride as a little team.

I find it interesting how frequently solo mums refer to the traditional roles of mother and father: that they are both nurturing and providing for their child or children. I do it myself. A lot of it is shorthand: solo mums don't subscribe to such stereotypes, as they're busy breaking them. But I feel that it shows that the language surrounding modern parenting hasn't caught up with reality, whether that's words for genetic half-siblings or relationships with donors, or words for parenting. I suspect most fathers and mothers I know would be deeply offended not to be recognised for the nurturing they do of their children.

I'm curious to find out how being donor conceived has affected the lives of adults: is it, as Christelle feels, simply how they were made, or does it sometimes feel more, as if it's a part of them? I'm aware that many teenagers who have been told about their donor from close to birth wonder why their parents frequently bring up the subject of their genetic history when it holds no emotional weight – and is often of very little interest – to them.

I talk to a group of people in their twenties about being donor conceived. Ellie, twenty-eight, is totally open about her conception to everyone: all of her colleagues know where she's from. It's something she shares on first dates. She never hides anything, because she doesn't have anything to hide. She recommends that mums tell their children as early as possible so that there is never any shock in finding out about their origins. She also recommends surrounding children with other children, so that even if their home isn't always full of people, they feel rich in friendships. She also suggests encouraging children to be as open as possible: in her experience, if you tell people your history straight away then 'unless they're a total arsehole' they won't react. It makes it much harder for it to be a problem for them.

Ellie was brought up living with her mum in London. Her admiration and respect for her mum is amazing to hear about. I wonder if their relationship is so strong partly because of the absence of a father in Ellie's life. I hope that this is an advantage of being part of a solo-parent family that Astrid and I will benefit from.

Her mum's fertility treatment involved so many trips to clinics that she ended up buying a dry ice freezer on wheels, in which she'd take sperm home from the clinic to use at the appropriate time.

While the shift to ban anonymity in sperm donors was, I believe, a positive for our society, it had unexpected negative effects for Ellie's mum, who was thirty-nine when she had her daughter. She desperately wanted to have more children through the same sperm donor, but this became impossible when the law changed. She was hesitant about using a different donor, and by the time she'd reflected on it she felt too much time had passed.

Ellie's mum, who has had a successful career, explained to Ellie when she was tiny that she was here because she was so very wanted. But this left some confusion in Ellie's mind. She went to a Catholic primary school when she was very young, despite their family not being Catholic, and was bullied about where her father was. People would tell her that her mother was a Virgin Mary. Then, when she was six, on a drive to France on holiday, her mother explained to her about where she came from. And at last Ellie felt happy, rather than confused.

From that moment, she felt clear about her origins and was always very open about them. She didn't want anyone to tiptoe around them imagining a dead dad or absent father. She wasn't bullied again.

She feels hugely positive about her family set-up. She has six godparents who are all incredibly supportive, and has always had a really good relationship with her mum. She regards her three godfathers as quasi father figures, and they have been wonderful to her.

As she was growing up, Ellie's mum always told her daughter that her role of solo mum meant that she could raise her in the way she believed to be best. She had watched her friends bicker over bedtimes and schools, and felt very lucky:

if she wanted to keep Ellie out later than usual, or cuddle up to her in bed, there was nobody to object or complain. Ellie says her mum has never admitted to her that there were any downsides, although she imagines that there must have been some. I admire her mum for being open about the positives of being a solo mum. I too want Astrid to know how lucky I feel to get to spend so much time with her.

Ellie disarms me when she admits that when she watches films such as *Mamma Mia*, or *What a Girl Wants*, which is centred on a daddy–daughter dance, she finds she gets very upset. She is secure that she was very wanted by her mum, and believes children are far more damaged by their parents splitting up than not having a dad to begin with. I feel she's brave to mention this pang. I wonder if, however balanced and open and proud any donor-conceived child is of their origins, there will always be a question of how it would have felt to have a dad when growing up. I imagine that every solo mum experiences the paradox of wanting to take any upset away, while also knowing that they wouldn't change their child and it is a part of them.

There have been two occasions when people have upset Ellie hugely with comments about how she was born. Her former best friend once told her she'd be really selfish if she did the same thing as her mum, because Ellie's son or daughter would only have two members of their family. (They didn't fall out over this comment, it was later they stopped being friends.) For many years after, Ellie felt influenced by that remark and was put off the idea of becoming a single mum, but in reality she now feels she would follow that path if she wasn't in a relationship and wanted to conceive, as she definitely wants children.

The other negative comment came from Ellie's mum's one snooty friend. He didn't want her being friends with his son, because she didn't have a traditional background with a proper family tree.

Ellie's upbringing was happy, and she was always very close to her mum, but sometimes she wished there was a second person so that her mum wasn't working so hard, and sometimes she wished for a sibling so that even if her mum was working hard, Ellie would have company.

Now she's an adult working as a lawyer, Ellie believes she got her own ambition from seeing her mum work hard. And she doesn't yearn for a bigger family, because she loves her closeness to her mum.

Ellie is currently trying to find her family members. The clinic that provided the sperm promised her mum that she would be told the eye colour and profession of the donor when her daughter reached eighteen. But the clinic had shut down by then, so her mum applied for information from the Donor Conceived Register. Ellie has since signed up to Ancestry.com and 23andme.com, although no matches have been made to date.

Ellie recently went to a Donor Conceived Register meeting and says she found it much more upsetting than she'd anticipated. She sat, for the first time, in an entire room full of people who understood. Until the meeting, she'd never met anyone who was donor conceived. She hadn't realised how much bottled-up emotion she had surrounding her conception.

She knows that the chances of finding biological half-siblings are tiny, but she still hopes. 'All my family are quite short and I'm weirdly tall,' she says. A DNA-testing site has told her that she's got Scandinavian blood, and she'd like to find those features in someone else. 'If I find the donor, that would be great. I'm not looking for a father or a best friend, but I am curious.' But she's aware that she doesn't want the

search to become a big focus in her life, because she doesn't
want it to overtake how happy she is – and how much she
admires her mum. It's so heartening to see how proud she is
of her origins. No one can attack her for being donor conceived, because she doesn't see it as a weakness in any way. I
hope I help Astrid feel as loved and secure as Ellie.

Ellie is so loyal towards her mum, and so open about her
respect, admiration and appreciation of her that I'm left
hopeful that Astrid might one day feel similarly towards
me. I wonder how much having one parent has helped make
Ellie and her mother especially close – and whether an upside
of being a solo parent is frequently a stronger relationship
between parent and children.

I immediately notice a similar love and respect from
Miranda to her mum, whom I meet for a cup of tea in north
London. She is twenty-five and, unusually in the early 1990s,
her donor did not request anonymity. But this didn't make
her search for her genetic family pain-free. She felt she was
betraying her mum when she decided to search for her half-
siblings and donor.

Her mum had the name of the clinic written on a Post-it
note, and a piece of paper with basic information about the
donor: the subject he studied, his weight and height. She
asked for the information, but the clinic had shut down,
so she contacted the Human Fertilisation and Embryology
Authority, who looked through all their paper files from
the clinic on her behalf. They found information about her
donor, and within a few months had passed it on to her, with
the offer of counselling.

Miranda became curious about her donor and wanted
to know what he looked like. Once she'd seen a picture of
him, she thought her curiosity would be satisfied, but then
she wanted to go on to meet him.

They started getting to know each other; they went to exhibitions and out for coffee.

She found that their lifestyles were worlds apart although they live in the same city: he is very wealthy, has a massive family and a huge house, a wife and children. Whereas her family is artistic and everyone believes in following their passion, his family is money-focused and have pursued careers that are considered conventionally successful. They saw each other frequently, and then it started to feel a bit much, perhaps for both of them. He said he felt bad that he wasn't around while she was growing up, but this felt confusing because she wouldn't have wanted him around when she was growing up. He seemed to want to step into a dad role that he felt was missing from her life, and on numerous occasions she'd remind him that she had both a mum and a dad, just in one body, and that her mum filled both those roles. He also confided in Miranda that his wife was finding the situation of discovering a genetic relation awkward, which made her feel very uncomfortable.

The whole experience was highly emotionally charged, not least because on some level she felt that she was betraying her mum with her interest in him. It was only after meeting her donor that she told her mum about it, and she says that if they'd met only once, or if she'd found it an unpleasant meeting, perhaps she would never have mentioned it. But as they met several times, she decided to tell her. It wasn't easy to broach the subject, and she's sure that she hurt her mum.

'I have to think of myself as well,' she says. 'I never want her to think she wasn't enough – because she was – and that's not why I wanted to meet him or contact him.' She wanted to know who he was and what he looked like, but she never felt that she needed another parent figure in her life. 'I should tell my mum that more,' she says.

She joined the Donor Sibling Registry and found out that

she is one of five half-siblings, a group of two men and three women – so far. One of her half-siblings is just two and a half weeks older than her.

Miranda has learnt that these relations have become her biological family simply by chance: in the early 1990s the clinic receptionists would keep a note of all the donors who came in, and team up prospective mothers with their donors by similarity of looks.

She's become close to one of her half-sisters, who is about to embark on fertility treatment and sperm donation herself with her partner. But Miranda says that it's a very different relationship to the one she has with her brother with whom she grew up, although technically she shares as much blood with each of them, as he was born by a different donor. So much is about growing up together: she doesn't look on her half-sister as a sibling in the same way.

Now, she feels slightly anxious that there might be more half-siblings out there, as she doesn't really feel the need to find more.

When Miranda was growing up, she always knew she was donor conceived – and she feels grateful that this wasn't information that she discovered later in her life. In primary school, she felt embarrassed when questioned about whether she had a dad and would say that she didn't know where he was. If people would press for answers, she'd say that he left when she was very young. She just wanted to shut down the conversation and found it effective.

In her first year of secondary school, she told one person, a really close friend, and explained what a donor meant to her. But she didn't tell anyone else, and by then would simply say to people: 'No, I don't have a dad.' Some teachers and students would say that she must do, and so she'd tell them that he died or he left, making it up on the fly.

She says that even the word 'sperm', when you're eleven, sounds a bit strange, and she found the whole subject incredibly awkward. I wonder about the difference in approach when growing up between her and Ellie, and suspect that Ellie's upfront attitude stops any awkwardness. I imagine that so much is dependent both on the character of the two women and also the people they are surrounded by as they grow up. I hope that by being open I encourage Astrid to feel confident rather than uncomfortable, and that we continue to live in areas where people are accepting of alternative family set-ups.

Miranda feels that she's developed a front and has chosen to ignore the questioning. It could have upset her and become a big issue in her life, she believes, but instead she decided to just get on with it. She wonders whether she might have inherited that resilience from her mum, who became a solo mum at a time when sperm donation was so much rarer and less talked about. Many people may have presumed her children were products of one-night stands, which isn't accurate, and Miranda speculates that this might have upset her when she went through rounds of sperm donation in order to have children. Even walking into a clinic alone must have been really hard.

Today, Miranda feels that many more people understand about donors, and society has started to catch up with women's decisions. As an adult, no one cares about her upbringing: she chats about her mum a lot in work, but people are far less likely to directly question her about her dad. I feel relieved that she feels that society is evolving and wonder if her embarrassment and shying away from questions about a dad is because the emphasis on conformity was so much stronger two decades ago.

She doesn't feel at all embarrassed now, but she does think

that if her mum had kept it a secret she'd have found it hard. And she finds that having met her donor was a relief. When she thinks of starting a family herself, it's reassuring to know her family history and particularly about her father's health.

Miranda believes that being donor conceived will affect how she parents. If she finds she can't have children, she will definitely consider using donor sperm or eggs. She's seen her mum do more than two parents in bringing up her and her brother, helping them both follow their passions and being involved with both of their lives, so she would not be put off parenthood by being single.

And she gives me advice in parenting Astrid, saying that the most important thing is to be open with her. She tells me not to be upset or offended if she wants to know more, but says that the whole topic must have been more of a shock to her mum, because it was unexpected, than for my generation where donors are identifiable. She's relieved that the law has changed, and feels she'd be more confident using a donor now she knows that a child's curiosity can routinely be satisfied. She helps me to understand how important the quest for identity is for some people who are donor conceived. I hope that I can initiate these conversations with Astrid, pass on information to her about her donor and suggest that if ever it's something she wants to explore as an adult, I'm there to help in any way, whether that's to listen to her thoughts or to plan a family holiday to the US if she ever arranges to meet her donor for a coffee.

Miranda says that no donor-conceived children should worry about asking questions or wondering about their background: it's perfectly normal.

I feel grateful to have met such strong, loving adults. If Astrid has as good a relationship with me as they have with their mothers, we too will be a very lucky family. And however she chooses to approach the issue of her genetic background with other people, I'll be there to share it with her and support her.

14

A Year of Astrid

Astrid and I form a little team together, but she's also becoming an individual with her own preferences – and demands. Nursery is the first, tiny step along the path to independence for her. And to do the very best by her, I realise that it's important for me to reclaim elements of my own independence too, which is a long-winded way of saying that I joined a dating website.

Now, my history of dating isn't great, unless the person is already a friend. I frequently have crushes, but a friend of mine has described them, lovingly, as 'unrealistic'. I wonder whether this might have changed in a world with Astrid.

I certainly feel less likely to rush into anything. There's no time pressure any more, as I'm not racing against dwindling fertility. And I'm sleep deprived, which makes me less focused on dating. Even most people I know with partners would choose an amazing night of sleep over a date with their husband or boyfriend after almost a year of interrupted nights, so I feel I'm in good company.

I no longer have time to mess around with someone who isn't open to a serious relationship, but equally, I'm very content not to be in a relationship too. I'm also not sure whether I would be able to give someone new any significant time in my life, so perhaps I'm not really available, for now. I'm aware that I've been a little bit unlucky when it comes to dating in my thirties; and I've had some wonderful relationships too. But now I feel protective of my daughter first and foremost.

In the months after my miscarriage with Seth, hoping for distraction from feeling miserable, I joined a group to help build a lido in south-east London. I went for dinner a couple of times with the man heading up the outside swimming effort, but nothing happened, and within a few months he had a new partner, who quickly got pregnant.

I next bumped into him at my local play club, and found out that he'd split up with his girlfriend. It sounded as if he'd had a harrowing time, but watching him play with his daughter, it seemed clear that he was a great, loving dad.

With my mum tum and baby weight, I didn't feel my most confident, but I got up my courage and asked him out.

'We should go for dinner sometime,' I suggest, blushing hugely.

'Yes, there's a place nearby I've been thinking about going to,' he tells me.

'Great, my mum is always up for babysitting,' I say.

'Oh, well, shall we go early and bring the kids,' he adds.

And at that moment I knew he saw me only as a friend. Which is great in itself. I swallowed a couple of times, then replied: 'Yes, that sounds great.'

A week later I check whether we're meeting up with our children, but he's busy. I realise that he was probably just being polite. We continue to catch up each week at the local community play club, and the self-consciousness I feel wears off quickly – a few rounds of 'The Wheels on the Bus' and my clumsy approach to dating seems forgotten.

I download a dating app, but I find it hard to feel any enthusiasm, and wonder if it might be just a little early. Astrid is teething and, subsequently, my idea of a good night involves a lot of pyjamas.

I do go on one date with a lawyer whose children are just about to start secondary school. He talks lots about coaching them to get into a grammar school, and about his ex-wife's lack of ambition since having children. I've never met her, but I feel like he's being harsh. We have an entertaining evening: once I've arranged for my mum to babysit there's no way that I'm going to call time after one drink. In this way, I feel more ready for online dating than before having Astrid, when I'd rush home as soon as I'd established we weren't going to grow old together, preferring my housemates' company to that of an unknown date. But I don't think that either the lawyer or I would want to spend any more time together.

I focus on my daughter and work, and occasionally swipe left and right on dating apps, more for my self-esteem than because I want to act on anything. I decide that a relationship will come along in its own time.

In the meantime, I navigate my return to work. Since becoming a mum, I've found a new-found calm confidence in every piece I've written and project I've worked on. I don't have time for self-doubt, which I think makes my work so much better that it quickly becomes a virtuous circle. Wonderful offers start coming my way. I feel that with Astrid around I shine both with her and when I am working. My ambition bubbles up as a sense of responsibility to provide for my daughter.

I decide to minimise my commute and concentrate on

copywriting at a technology and design studio that I've worked for frequently over the years. They offer flexible hours and I'm impressed that the general manager – a new dad – starts our conversation with a question of whether I am looking for two or three days, rather than pushing me for a full-time position.

I also start writing a newspaper column on life as a solo mum, filling in for a columnist on a short break, which I love, and writing for the newspaper when time allows.

The Human Fertilisation and Embryology Authority releases figures saying that the number of people having children alone doubled between 2009 and 2016, and a right-wing columnist writes a piece saying that solo mothers are selfish. She says that if we want affection we should 'get a cat'. Aside from being pulled up for her obvious lack of understanding of the nature of cats, the piece manages to upset many solo mums. I feel that it was written to create a reaction, rather than out of any deeply held point of view or true concern for society, and I write a heartfelt response.

Magazines approach me asking for stories about bringing up my daughter as a single mum.

Each time I write, women get in touch to let me know that it's a decision they're considering, or to express their support. Some are young women who ask whether it's too soon for them to choose to have a child alone or if they should wait. Others are older and ask whether or not they should go solo. I can't answer their questions, I can only tell them about my experiences, and I find myself frequently saying how useful I found counselling. I ask them all to update me; I so want to hear what they decide and how they find being a solo mum, if they follow that path.

Other women get in touch saying they're pregnant, and one soon-to-be grandfather writes to say his daughter is about to give birth as a solo mum. It's wonderful that people are happy to contact me and share their experiences, and I feel proud that I'm talking about a subject that seems to be on many single women's minds.

I'm in our local play club with Astrid one morning when a woman introduces herself as a life coach. We're chatting about returning to work and she offers me some advice.

'I don't want to be intrusive,' she tells me. 'But there's one thing I was told when I had my first child, and it's the best piece of advice I've received.' I'm curious. 'Never say you've got baby brain,' she advises. 'It's fine around friends, but never in a work context. Half the people in any office are overtired, hungover, or just stayed up late watching a film. You don't need to ever make excuses.'

I take her advice.

As friends start negotiating hours to return to work with their employers – one leaving her job because they wouldn't be flexible enough to let her work four and a half days a week instead of five – I feel exceptionally lucky.

Before starting my new job, I move Astrid's cot into her own room. It's almost unused; most of the time we end up cuddling in bed together. A friend whose daughter is a few months younger than Astrid has recently done the same thing, and she's telling me that her daughter now sleeps through the night. I'm shattered, and this sounds like an oasis in a sleep desert. She offers to help carry the cot with me, and we set it up in Astrid's new room.

That night, I read Astrid her bedtime stories, but she doesn't sleep, so I tell her that I love her and leave the room, and she cries. Many friends have successfully sleep-trained their children, but they have partners who they presumably turn to when they feel guilty hearing – and ignoring – the cries of their child.

A few minutes later, I go back in. I keep following this pattern, going in and out, reassuring Astrid how much I love her while feeling wretched. Eventually she sleeps.

I follow the same pattern for the next two nights, and Astrid's sleeping improves. Then she gets a fever, and I bring her back into bed with me so that I can keep her close. Over the next months, she spends some nights in her cot, and many in bed with me. It's something I know I wouldn't be doing nearly so frequently if I had a partner – I'd want us to have shared time together. But, in those first weeks of nursery and my return to work, it seems to provide us both with comfort.

I still get to spend most of my time with my smiley daughter, and the pleasure of being with her fills my weeks. My eyes wrinkle up when I smile, and Astrid's are exactly the same: every morning we exchange giant, wrinkly-eyed smiles. She's also inherited my laugh, and will giggle uncontrollably if we play peekaboo, or if I bend her legs so her toes touch her nose. She loves to make me laugh too, and when she realises she's doing something funny – like trying to fill up a cup in a bath while holding it upside down – she looks delighted and keeps doing it to get the same reaction again.

I'm frequently told that Astrid is an 'easy' baby; she will amuse herself as well as wanting me to entertain her. She goes through very clingy phases where she won't leave my side, and I sometimes resort to peeing with her on my knee because it saves her wailing from a different room, but bathroom privacy aside, she is utterly joyful. She loves exploring the world, and I can see her changing almost daily as she becomes more aware and able to do new things, which she applauds herself for learning. She loves attention, and if family or friends come to visit she will involve each and every one in her applause. We hold each other tight when we cuddle, and Astrid approaches people she loves and bends her head towards them, hoping for a hug or a kiss.

I'm also aware that she might become more demanding as she grows older. Astrid is all-consuming now, and looking after her won't involve the constant vigilance as she becomes more independent, but her worries and fears will go beyond where her next bottle of milk is coming from. As she navigates her way to adulthood through a swiftly changing world, I'll have to sit on my hands, willing the world to smile back at her crinkly eyes and wishing I could make all her wishes come true. And observing her first heartbreak and disappointments along the way, hoping that she is a more grounded teenager than I was.

*   *   *

As Mother's Day approaches, I expect to feel a twinge that I'm not in a traditional home where, on one Sunday in March, I have a lie-in until I'm awoken with breakfast in bed. I hope that even in the most disappointing of partnerships, where resentment has replaced romance, that Mother's Day is marked.

But while I might not have a partner to create a Mother's Day celebration for me, other people step in. First up, Astrid makes a card at nursery. Her handprint in orange paint, alongside a photo of her with some scrunched-up tissue. I love it so much that I can't look at it when her nursery teacher passes it over to me, along with a single rose stem, in case she sees the emotion in my face.

Then, the day before Mother's Day I receive a card in the mail. I find motherhood and mail are not easy bedfellows and have struggled to keep up with correspondence since having Astrid, so I'm very picky about what post I get so far as opening: anything that looks unexciting gets added to an ever-growing pile, while anything addressed to Astrid gets opened immediately. But this printed card stands out because it's postmarked from Guernsey. Inside, it has a photo of me and Astrid, and a message from my daughter thanking me for bringing her into the world, saying I'm the kindest, coolest, funniest Mama ever, and that she especially enjoys our morning cuddles and swimming, and is looking forward to going on adventures with me. By the time I've read it, tears are streaming down my face. I spend some time tracking down the sender, until my friend Bec tells me it's all Astrid's work. I love that she's thought how much it would mean to me.

I enjoy walking Astrid round the park on the Sunday morning of Mother's Day to help her to nap. It's crowded and there are more dads than mums out with their children.

My family comes over for lunch; my mum and grandmother offering flowers, my brother, nephews and Astrid creating a lively afternoon of tower building, bowling and banging wooden spoons. I might not have got a traditional Mother's Day lie-in, but I feel lucky all day. And when my mum explains to my nephews that every woman around the table is a mummy, I'm quick to point out that it was a close-run thing with me and I'm lucky to have got in before it was too late. I wonder whether this might prompt my nephews to ask about Astrid's daddy – I keep waiting for their questions – but they don't really seem to have noticed. Perhaps in another couple of years? Or maybe I'm possibly expecting questions when none are needed? Perhaps it's just normal to them. Most children I know are accepting of whatever they see in front of them, and aren't affected by societal norms and structures. They are no more likely to question the absence of a father figure than the presence of a bunny that brings Easter eggs in spring or a bearded man who fills stockings: everything is possible and there is no such thing as 'normal'.

I get my lie-in a few weeks later: my mum comes and spends a few nights at mine to give me a chance to sleep properly. The choppy nights are catching up with me, as my daughter's fifth and sixth teeth are giving her grief, and I feel like I've hit a wall of tiredness.

I cancel a night out with a friend because I feel that adding anything more into my life would be too much for me at that moment: I desperately want to catch up with my friend, but I don't have the energy to chat, and I don't want to drink in case I feel hungover the next day. And so, instead of babysitting while I go out, my mum babysits so that I can stay in. She puts Astrid to bed, reading her bedtime stories and singing her songs. She might be Astrid's only grandparent, but she gives the love of four. I run round our flat and give it a swift tidy. I have a baby monitor in my bedroom so that I can see and hear if Astrid's upset in the night. But when my mum stays, instead of waking up and crying, which she does for me, she wakes up and is silent. I am baffled but delighted. And while 7.30am would never have felt like a lie-in before having Astrid, it feels like complete luxury to wake up and slowly come round, then to go upstairs to see my daughter playing contentedly with her teddy and my mum.

A week before her first birthday, Astrid stands unsupported for a couple of seconds – the string from a walk-along toy in one hand the only thing keeping her steady. Tears spring to my eyes as I shower her with praise. I'm so happy to witness these moments, and I think how amazing it would be to have someone with whom to share them. Ideally, with their phone at the ready to film anything significant. There will be many more to come: starting school, nativity plays and sports days, all steps towards independence. I'm lucky that I have family and close friends who I've no doubt will share an interest in these pivotal moments in Astrid's and my life. But I imagine these are moments that are beautiful to share with a partner. I'll never feel like I stand out attending alone when many parents are unable to make these events at all, and I feel that this has to be an advantage of working for a flexible company, and of being an older mum – I'm experienced enough at my job to take time off for these firsts in Astrid's life. Hopefully, I'll be able to give a cheer for some of my daughter's pals too whose parents are unable to get the time off work.

My only sadness is that my dad is unable to be here to join in the delight of watching my daughter grow: I think he'd love to see her take on the world. I'm very glad that he met my nephew William, with whom he shares a name.

When Astrid was tiny, I thought that I would arrange a big naming-day celebration for her on her first birthday. If I went to church for more than just the nativity service, I'd get her christened, but I wasn't exactly sure how to qualify, or whether it was meddling when I want her to make up her own mind about religion and politics, so a secular naming ceremony seemed a great way to celebrate.

But during the course of the last year, I've learnt that being a solo mum is more about keeping up with today than planning ahead (or at least it is for me – I'm sure there are some ultra-organised parents who cast their mind beyond the next twenty minutes). So the grand celebration is replaced by plans for a party at the community play club, which Astrid loves.

I buy her a ball pit for her birthday with hundreds of white, grey, blue and pink balls, perfect for the party and a good bedroom toy afterwards. A cardboard Wendy house with sheets of stickers and crayons for decorating its walls will, I hope, make a good activity for the older children. I order platters of sandwiches and pick up bottles of Prosecco. My nephews – and their mum – bake an amazing cake for

Astrid with the neatest letter A formed out of sweets. On the morning of Astrid's birthday, I pick up helium balloons to decorate the play club, and to give to children to take home with them when they leave.

In the week leading up to Astrid's birthday I feel emotional thinking that this time a year ago I was willing her to get a wriggle on. At 2pm, just as the party starts, I think this is the time I first met my daughter. But as we start celebrating, I can't think of anything other than how lovely it is to share the occasion with friends and family. I look around and see Lucinda, whom I've known since I was five, with her family; friends who I studied my journalism degree with; neighbours and local mothers whom I've met since having Astrid; Michele, my doula, who was sprinkling lavender essential oil exactly a year before; and my nephews, brother and sister-in-law and my mum. These people are such a big part of Astrid's and my world, they've seen us through the last twenty-one months.

We play a game of pass the parcel, which is hugely ambitious for the babies. Many lose interest and crawl off, leaving their parents passing the newspaper-wrapped layers around the circle. The day goes in a series of wonderful moments. One is when my eldest nephew explains to everyone the rules to pass the parcel and warns everyone, 'No cheating!' Another, when one boy opens his parcel layer to find a bath toy, which he looks at in disgust and throws into the circle, so pleasingly honest in his disappointment and disinterest. Another, watching my youngest nephew decorate the Wendy house with the help of one of my friends. And my favourite: seeing my daughter's face confused then delighted as she tries chocolate cake for the first time.

One of the mums at Astrid's first birthday party is Saskia, whom I first met at pregnancy yoga and whose daughter will turn one in a few weeks. We still meet up regularly, and I love the thought that our children will be in touch as they grow older and will know that there are many other families out there that don't conform to the mum-and-dad model.

I ask Saskia what has surprised her about the first year of being a team with her daughter. She says that the major thing that has struck her is how much love she feels. The hard times aren't as hard as she expected because they're powered by an intense drive to make this little being as happy and comfortable as possible.

Before she had her daughter, she remembers inviting her many friends with children over for dinner and offering to cook for them so that they could have a break from their kids. When she offered, she'd never understood that they wouldn't have felt any resentment towards their children. Nor just how much they loved them.

The extreme levels of tiredness that come with parenting have also taken her by surprise: the compounded tiredness that parents feel in their bones after being awoken every night for months on end. Spiritually, if she had a babysitter she'd love to go for a big night out with friends, but the reality is that a big part of her would be wondering how she'd cope with it.

Saskia's first months with her daughter were terrifying. On their way home from hospital her newborn baby stopped breathing and lost consciousness. She and her dad turned straight back round to hospital. After a week under the care of doctors and nurses, they were discharged with the suggestion that it might have been because the angle of car seats doesn't support new babies. Once her dad had dropped the new family to their home in south-east London, Saskia felt petrified that her daughter would stop breathing in her sleep and she wouldn't be awake to look after her. Her mum helped her out by paying for a night nanny to come and look after the pair of them, and give Saskia the chance to sleep and recover from her Caesarean section rather than constantly feeling anxious about her daughter's health.

A couple of weeks later, her daughter stopped breathing again, and Saskia was terrified that she was going to lose her. She felt alone in hospital with no one to get her a cup of tea, although the care she received from the nurses was amazing. She found it worrying not having anyone else with her when consultants were passing on information. She wished that there was someone with whom she could check over what was said. The immense responsibility weighed heavily, and she was utterly exhausted, but adrenalin saw her through: there was no way she was going to let her daughter down when she was so vulnerable.

She felt very protective of her daughter, but over the months she proved herself to be resilient, and Saskia is now very relaxed with her.

There have only been a few times that Saskia's cried since becoming a mum, but one was when her daughter was struggling with acid reflux and in pain. Saskia would give her medicine every three hours and have to hold her upright after each feed. Her daughter cried for so long one night that she remembers feeling completely overwhelmed, and she too started crying. I ask whether she felt lonely, but she says that it was instead a feeling of helplessness – that she couldn't take the pain away – that made it tough. The following day she pleaded with her doctor to investigate, and they found out that her daughter was dairy intolerant. Things changed dramatically once she cut lactose from her diet.

Saskia found weaning surprisingly stressful: she's never heard anyone say that it's a challenge, and she wasn't warned to brace herself for the merry-go-round of preparing food for her daughter, feeding and cleaning up. But that was nothing compared with returning to work, which she found heart-breaking. She asked her friends why they hadn't warned her how awful it feels to leave your baby, and they said there was no point: it wouldn't have made it feel any better to be fore-warned. She talked through all her childcare decisions with friends who have used nannies, childminders and nurseries, and found this more useful – she suspects – than a partner who was as new to it all as she is.

She frequently appreciates being able to make the deci-sions about what is best for her daughter, and doesn't have to compromise with a partner who might have strong, yet conflicting, views to her own.

Another advantage she finds to solo parenting is that her free time is her own. 'I know the point of a relationship is that you really want to spend time with that person, but I'd also want some time on my own,' she says. 'And I don't know how easy that is in a couple when there is a small child involved.' She feels that she has little energy left over for other people. Her friends are understanding of this, but in a relationship she is concerned that she'd feel she is failing at something. Instead, it feels a luxury to freely prioritise her daughter – though she's aware that she could be in a relationship that allowed her to stay at home to look after her daughter, so then she'd get to spend more time with her.

The one sadness she feels is that she's increasingly aware that her daughter doesn't have a dad. Saskia spends time with a lot more women than men, and she feels a melancholy that her daughter might have an imbalanced view of gender. She's starting to prepare herself for the 'why don't I have a daddy?' questions as she realises these aren't so far off any more. I too am aware that while I want to give the world to Astrid, this is the one thing I haven't given her. And while I'm delighted that we make a wonderful family, I'm sorry about that.

When I hear children saying, 'Daddy! Daddy!' at nursery I wonder whether she ever questions why she doesn't have a daddy. And if she starts saying dada when she's playing in the bath, or if we're snuggling together, and I'm not sure what she's trying to tell me, I'll often take the moment to explain that she has a mummy, and a grandma called Addie, and an uncle Henry and an auntie Jess, and two cousins William and Dylan, and how much we all love her – but that she doesn't have a daddy.

* * *

When I started to write about my journey to try to become a mother, I thought it would be a story about how life doesn't always follow a predictable path; or of how life isn't quite how I imagined it would be at school, when inspirational speakers would come in for big assemblies; or how I imagined it while I was lying in the arms of lovers, thinking I'd found home. But it's better than that. Now that Astrid's in my world, I realise just *how* much better: she's the best, most wonderful person that could ever have come into my life. I wouldn't change anything, because everything has led to her.

As she turns one, I'm left to reflect on the year that has passed, and the year before, when I grew her inside me. And I can't imagine a world without her. I can't believe that in just one orbit of the sun she's gone from a tiny girl with a cry that sounded like a baby sparrow to an almost-toddler who knows exactly what she wants, and isn't afraid to voice it. She's gone from baths in the kitchen sink to lying back on a baby bath chair in the bath to now crawling and climbing around on the fish-patterned bath mat.

She flatters me by finding me funny: when I say 'Oh!', as

bubbles I blow pop, she thinks it's hilarious; when I'm hoping to get her dressed in the morning and she crawls away and I crawl after her and she thinks we're playing the best game; when I put my sunglasses on her and she thinks I've cracked a brilliant joke. I too find her funny: she leans around the side of sofas and doors playing her own, more amusing, version of hide-and-seek, and has learnt 'uh oh' as one of her first words, which she uses to comedic effect, often after throwing toys on the floor so that she gets more chances to voice it. She's started lifting up her hands to me when she sees me and wants to be picked up.

I think she sees us as equals. She's become dextrous when it comes to feeding herself and now tries to feed me if ever I offer her food.

She loves pushing and trying to throw balls – we spend hours passing them back and forth to each other. She loves pulling herself up and hasn't quite learnt to balance on her two tiny feet so she will use anything, from my hair to a piece of furniture, to keep herself steady. And she loves a cuddle and to be held close.

I find it hard to take her to nursery, but I know she enjoys playing with the other children – and playing with paint and sand and water baths. Far worse is the sense of guilt when I'm with her but distracted. When my eyes flick to my mobile, as someone pings a message through. She too is intrigued by this contraption where I seem to store people who I bring out on the screen to wave to her, and where she knows – already – that she can find animated nursery rhymes. I resolve that I'll check my phone at the beginning, middle and end of the day, rather than attempting to keep up with conversations.

I can't wait to see her grow and find out what she's interested in, to be able to understand the animated conversations that she's trying to have, to watch and admire as she becomes more independent and finds her own way through this won-derful world.

* * *

There are a few things that I've learnt along the way. The last year has gone incredibly quickly: an oxytocin-rich cuddle bubble, a blur of sleep deprivation. Parenthood paves the path in front of me, and I know it gets a lot harder as chil-dren get older. I'm still a novice parent and it's going to be a steep learning curve as I learn how to bring up a happy, secure child. Here are a few things I've learnt so far about solo parenting:

Responsibility can be a mixed blessing A friend recounted an argument with her partner about introducing new foods into their son's life (a psychologist might suspect it wasn't really a row about food). I constantly make tiny decisions on Astrid's behalf: which shampoo; whether to pick organic food; plastic, metal or bamboo cutlery. I'd find it tricky to keep checking if someone else is happy with these micro choices. But then there are big, weighty decisions: which nursery she'll be happiest at, whether to rush her to A&E when her temperature's peaking at 40 degrees, where I'd love a second opinion. A group of friends who are happy to talk through big choices, whatever time of night, is invaluable for a solo parent.

Accept kindness and help Whether it's a bag of clothes or an offer to help move a cot, I'm learning to say yes please to help. It's liberating, I frequently feel very grateful, and it means I don't end up sobbing because Ikea flat packs are beyond me.

*

There's a reason there's a time limit to Sainsbury's car parks Babies fall asleep at inopportune moments. And depending on how much sleep I've had in the last 48 hours, I might not want to interrupt it. So, yes, if I arrive at Sainsbury's with a sleeping Astrid, I will sometimes join her in shutting my eyes – and taking a total of three hours to buy a couple of pints of milk.

There will be times you'll wish you have someone to share your child with When my daughter started to crawl, I felt overwhelmed with pride and joy. I know that in the next few days, she'll take her first steps. I can't wait. I'm fully aware that there's no one in the world who'll feel the wonder that I do (though Astrid likes to applaud herself, which I love). Exceptional experiences are always great to share, and, although I'm surrounded by brilliantly supportive friends and family, I suspect sharing memorable moments with a partner feels particularly lovely.

Solo parenting is not for perfectionists Before Astrid, my life frequently felt slightly chaotic: juggling lots while hoping for the best. I wasn't a stranger to being late, or forgetting things. Now, I'm far more organised than I've ever been and still I am sometimes late and forget things. Being a perfectionist and a solo mum would be a tricky combination – it's a comfort to accept that life is sometimes beyond my control.

Keep a supply of batteries I had no idea that I'd spend roughly a quarter of my time changing toy batteries and that they come in odd sizes like C. Prospective parents: create a battery drawer.

Things my daughter does will move me more than anything else has in my life Not just big milestones. The first time she uses a crayon to make a faint mark on paper, her first drawing, I was moved beyond belief.

It's okay to have doubts I've never, for even one second, doubted that having my daughter is the very best thing to happen in my life. By anyone's standards, Astrid was an easy baby; as long as she was cuddled she was happy, which suited me. But I know many, many women who have wondered what they've done, both in couples and alone. I know people who've spent huge amounts of time considering whether to have a child or not, who are completely floored when their newborn cries for hours on end each night, or who miss their previous life more than they imagined. These feelings are normal. Anyone whose baby cries for hours on end is going to go at least slightly out of their mind. And it's okay to question whether it's all a huge mistake.

The most important thing is to voice them, to share them with other mothers, because many will appreciate the honesty when experiencing similar feelings.

There's a simplicity to being a solo parent I floated through the first months of motherhood in a blissful, sleep-deprived haze, cuddling and nursing my daughter. My responsibility was to her alone, and it was magical.

Many friends have found it much harder with another relationship to maintain: they didn't feel that they could go to bed at 8pm (or would feel guilty if they did), and consequently would be shattered.

My daughter comes first. She's my favourite person and she has my attention. I don't mourn a changed relationship with my partner, or miss any former shared freedom. And there's a pleasurable straightforwardness to that.

Final Thoughts

I make a decision to try to make a sister or brother for Astrid before time runs out (if it hasn't already). I love the idea of her having a sibling friendship that lasts a lifetime and that certainly outlasts me. I know that being outnumbered will be tricky at times, but I'm up for the challenge. Practically, I might have to take a shorter maternity leave and work harder, but it will be worth it.

I go through insemination cycles, determined not to give too much focus to trying to get pregnant when Astrid is changing and growing each day, and I don't want to miss out on any of her. It feels different from when I was trying to get pregnant with Astrid, because she's in my world already. I'd love another child. I even start to feel wistful about pregnancy itself, which is ridiculous, because it surprised me hugely how much I didn't enjoy that nine months.

I find it amazing how quickly I slip back into buying tens of pregnancy tests, willing there to be a positive result. I spend time trying to second-guess whether I have symptoms that I'm creating a baby: is that a metallic taste in my mouth? Am I moody from sleep deprivation, or is there something more to it? Maybe my breasts just aren't achy because they're already fuller than they were when I was first pregnant with Astrid.

And the despondency I feel each month as my period comes. As each month passes, I realise how very fortunate I was to conceive Astrid: she feels more and more an unlikely miracle who came into my world.

I make peace with the frustrations of not getting pregnant when I go to see an osteopath, who says to me that there might be a positive to not expecting a sister or brother for Astrid to arrive imminently. 'Perhaps this is a gift you've given her: she gets to be a baby with all your attention for a little bit longer,' she says. And I am glad for that. As I write this, I'm considering whether to try IVF in the hope of making my daughter a sibling.

I expected that when Astrid started walking it would be a sudden thing, that she'd be a crawler one day and then a walker next. But the transformation is more gradual than that. First, a few faltering steps that my mum witnessed. Another week and she starts taking confident steps. My friend, Liz, has dropped round for a glass of wine after work. Astrid clings to me, then launches herself towards Liz, staggering as if she's the one with the wine. With cheers of encouragement, she staggers back to me. The praise, clapping and cheers keep her walking back and forth, her face beaming with joy and pride, long beyond her bedtime – I can't bear to put an end to her fun. That night, she sleeps well; the concentration and exertion have exhausted her.

She barely walks the next day, and takes just a few steps when I cheer her over the next couple of weeks. And then one day I see her practising. She starts walking from a table to a chair, steadying herself and looking delighted with her balance. Over the course of a couple of hours her confidence soars. After that, walking becomes her preferred way of getting around, holding her arms out to keep her balance, looking like the happiest zombie that has ever lived. Within weeks she's running and exploring and climbing.

I thought I'd feel emotional, and I'm right: I'm bursting with pride at my daughter taking her first steps. But I'd expected it to be a moment that felt slightly bittersweet, that I'd have wanted to share with someone who loved Astrid in the way I did. But, as it was, my mum, who adores her granddaughter, was there to share the first step, and Liz, whom Astrid adores, was there as she started to stagger. I didn't feel any wistfulness or wishing, simply lucky that Astrid is so surrounded by love.

As she starts to learn more words, I see them reflecting the important things in her world: teddy, bubbles, cheese, apple, shoes. And mummy, which I love and never tire of responding to, and daddy, instead of Addie, for her grand-mother, which is going to get awkward if it persists for long.

The week of Father's Day, Astrid makes me a card at nursery. 'I love you Mummy,' it says, written in the hand of one of her nursery carers. There's a photo of her and a handprint. On the outside it says Happy Day. The word Father has been covered in sticky stars. I love that I get two cards: it feels an acknowledgement that I do the work of both parents, and I'll keep it to show her when she's older.

On Father's Day itself, I take Astrid to the park early to go on the swings. I've never seen the children's playground so empty. There is only one other mum in the park – and even she is there by accident.

'I've never seen the park like this. Is it because it's Father's Day?' I ask.

'Argh, Father's Day,' she replies. 'I totally forgot.'

I explain that I'm a solo mum and my near neighbour, who lives a couple of streets away and who I've spoken to before at play club and in the park, tells me how much she admires me.

'It's so pragmatic,' she says. 'It just makes perfect sense.'

We chat about how different it is from Mother's Day, when the playground was full of dads who'd taken their children out, presumably leaving their partners to have a lie-in. I wonder if it's an illustration of different roles playing out: many mums still work shorter hours than their partners and spend more time with their children in the week, while many dads get to spend less time with their children. Whereas on Mother's Day, a treat might be a lie-in, on Father's Day people are presumably spending time with both parents. Except for those who forgot, or those who have small and wonderful families like mine and Astrid's.